# ANCHOR BOOKS

## *CENTRAL ENGLAND INSPIRATIONS 1999*

Edited by

Kelly Deacon

First published in Great Britain in 1999 by
ANCHOR BOOKS
Remus House,
Coltsfoot Drive,
Woodston,
Peterborough, PE2 9JX
Telephone (01733) 898102

HB ISBN 1 85930 740 X
SB ISBN 1 85930 745 0

# FOREWORD

Anchor Books is a small press, established in 1992, with the aim of promoting readable poetry to as wide an audience as possible.

We hope to establish an outlet for writers of poetry who may have struggled to see their work in print.

The poems presented here have been selected from many entries. Editing proved to be a difficult task and as the Editor, the final selection was mine.

*Anchor Books - Central England Inspirations 1999* is a compilation of poetry which has been assembled using the work of poets who reside in this area.

The poems vary in style and content, ranging from what they like about their town or city to pleasant memories in life and the joys of the world today.

Each poem is a unique inspiration reflecting on the true emotions from each poetic heart. A delightful collection for one and all to read time and time again.

I trust this selection will delight and please the authors and all those who enjoy reading poetry.

Kelly Deacon
Editor

# CONTENTS

## OBITUARY
### (Wife Resham Bi Yaqub departed 11 June 1991)

I cannot forget that hidden smile, by which once I was hooked.
I was astonished to find her more beautiful than she looked.

Nothing will separate us, we promised to stand by.
What a shame! You cannot live, I cannot die.

Perhaps fate grudged our selflessness in between,
Tearing apart souls, alas! it knew what it means?

When at half a century of my stolen past, I look,
I find your fingerprints on every page of my book.

It is not the death, it is my life now, that I dread.
Who will bother to feel, if I breathe or just lay dead?

I am looking forward to meeting you one day.
We will be together again in heaven, they say.

*M Yuquib Mirza*


## THE BALL

I've got this ball it bounced so high,
It bounced down our back yard,
It bounced round my mum's flowerbeds
And flattened all the heads.
I kicked it up and up it went,
I kicked it very high,
But then it came down again
And hit me in the eye.
And now I'm going in for tea
The ball can roll away.
'Cause I'm not going to play with it
Until another day.

*Kathy Watson*

# MY BUDGIE

In his cage my budgie sits proud
His squeaks and squawks are so very loud
He sips his water and eats his food
But only when he's in a good mood
He comes out of his cage
And sits on the windowsill
Sometimes he crashes and bashes his bill
He flies to the carpet all dazzled and dazed
I wonder if he'll recover, I'm really quite amazed
Then after a few seconds his feathers he shakes
And flies like the wind
No sound does he make
Back to his cage to recover from fright
As he settles down to rest for the night
Out goes the light, he sits quiet and still
Until the next morning, is he well or is he ill
From hitting his bill and falling to the floor?
Next time he will crash into the door
I wonder if he'll live to a ripe old age
He probably will if he stays in his cage.

*June Kennedy*


# THE GOOD OLD DAYS

It's nice to look back on those good old days,
But oh! how we've altered in so many ways,
I used to run up and down stairs, ducking a 39 bus,
But my! how the years take their toll on us.

When we are young, we're so full of zest,
Now we are older, we just do our best,
I walk up my hill, puffing away,
I could do with the energy I had yesterday.

But with the years I have mellowed, now I can laugh
So I'm not quite so nimble, and not quite so daft,
I now take my time, I don't rush around,
Because I now have my feet planted down on the ground.

I now have more time for the little things that matter,
I now have more time for a laugh and a natter,
Talking over old times, along with my friends,
The enjoyment it brings, cheers me no end.

*Eileen Handley*


## THE PLACE OF LEEK

In the shadow of ancient peaks
Isolated in rolling heather,
Defiant against vicious winter weather.
Yet receiver of crisp clean sun,
And a breeze of feathers.
Just as winter drove you to a tether.

Where Celtic Queens were crowned,
And English Kings sheltered safe and sound.
Where textiles made the pound,
And dwelling built for factory hounds.
The familiarity of nature's sounds,
In the woods we'd walk around.

Long talks,
Where the Churnet made her mark,
Childish larks,
Of rope swings and camp fire cracking bark.
Laugher and warm smoky beer smells
of many a pub after dark.

In the shadow of ancient peaks
Ancient people built the place of Leek.

*Terry Birch-Machin*

## SISTER - TO - SISTER

A sister is so precious by far the very best
To have one I am lucky, I feel I have been blessed.
The two of us are very close, together we belong.
You stand by me when I am right and support me when I'm wrong.
We both have our own problems but together we both try
To sort them out between us, to laugh and sometimes cry.
I know that you are always there if I should need a hand
You'll help me through the hardest times
From which life can command.
How I love you very much and admire all you do
And I'd like to say a 'thank you' for being only you.
And I will tell you here right now before this poem ends
I feel I have a sister who is my best and special friend.

*Glynis Whyke*

## LITTLE TERROR

Who broke my little dolly's arm
and smashed my favourite game?
I bet it was my brother
little terror is his name.
He's Mummy's little darling
he's always on her knee,
I hate my little brother
and I think that he hates me!
He messes up my jigsaws
And pulls my teddy's ear,
just wait till he is older
it's me he'll have to fear!

*Margaret Jean Wilcock*

# THE PANTHER

Panther, Panther
black as night
Panther, Panther
Out of sight!

He's out in the wild
he's in the cool
Leave him alone
Don't be a fool!

He's creeping along
the jungle floor
Then you hear his
Great big roar!

He then climbs up
His great big tree
look closely it's
Hard to see!

Now we're coming
near to the end
so say goodbye
to our friend
the
*Panther!*

***Jade Hughes  (13)***

## ANOTHER DAY

Dawn is breaking,
Birds are singing,
Thank you Lord for another day.

Mother Nature in all her glory,
Colour, flowers and earthly dew.
Thank you Lord for another day.

I awaken to greet yet another new day,
Joyous that I am still here to say;
'Thank you Lord for another day.'

Now is the time to pause, reflect and pray.
Life is too precious and I would love to stay.
Thank you Lord for another day.

*Shirley C Allen*


## HAS THE TRUST GONE?

Don't think you'll get near me now,
No one's coming close.
I won't ever feel fear now,
I'll be nobody's host.
You will never prey on me,
You will not make me sad.
Nobody can cause me harm,
I'll never get that lost, that bad.
Never trust a trusting face,
Then no one can desert me.
Safe and sound in my sweet world,
Where nobody can hurt me.

*Lynn Jean Barry*

# THE CRUSHED ROSE
*(Dedicated to my runaway daughter)*

Root of my soul loaned to me
A blessing for this earthly shell of mine
To have been given such a precious memory
A secret to nurture so divine
The formation of you was perfect
And fulfilment was complete
Oh the joy the exquisite joy
- And love that was taken for granted.
You were here. You had arrived
My lovely angel so much wanted
I helped you - watched you grow
Was so fond of you that I guess I tried too hard.
Your little life was being squeezed out of you.
By me. How was I to know?
Oh, I didn't know it, my sweetheart.
I loved you so much that I held you too tight
And as you grew you gasped for air
Your little shoots were all but stunted
By me, more and more, year by year.
But you were so beautiful all the same
I still didn't see the signs
'Til one day I looked and you had gone.
I retraced my steps - the way I had come
Searching for my precious flower
Back in mind's eye - in time - I pondered
Year by year - hour by hour
I wandered and I wandered
'Til finally I found it there - how only heaven knows
My prize, my lovely precious flower
Lying there - my own crushed rose.

*Jeanette M Tucker*

## SUFFOLK

The winding lane by flattened fields,
Tall trees and hedges standing.
Morning breaks and darkness yields,
With trawlers' catches landing.

The sudden change of vista
From countryside to sea,
Oh Suffolk, queen of counties
You mean so much to me.

The market place is central,
Kind faces, smiling friends all meet.
Well-kept homes and ordered stalls
Laid out in ancient street.

Where beach and coastline span.
Where things don't seem to change.
A fisher's hut, a stone crag.
As if since time began.

Wild flowers to crown each morning.
Sown crops sway in evening flow.
A moon to silhouette all standing things.
A place to love and know.

*D J Frost*

## LONELINESS

Don't be lonely, don't be afraid,
Because into the background you will fade.
Being on your own through trouble and fright,
People talking to you with hate and with spite.
Talking as if you were not there,
You try to speak they just don't care.
If they were in your place they may understand,
That now and again you need a little helping hand.

So don't be lonely, just try to cope,
Stand up with power, stand up with hope.
No more staring into empty spaced walls,
Shout your friends they may hear your calls.
Make them listen, make them hear,
Now you're not on your own through pain, through fear.

*Joanna Latham  (14)*


## HEAVEN FOUND

Boiling seas of passion rage
Within the faintest heart, waiting expectantly
To behold the glow of a
Fresh faced innocent that's comforting within
The hands of love

Thanks given when you're driven
Above the mortality of heartfelt desire
You're free from your cage of wire

Once again you fed the fire

The gentle touch and safety is yours
This tender clutch never do you
Want to leave
To stay suspended now and here
Would be a paradise in my dream

Her smiling face, radiating,
Shivers through your mind
In a daze, she is your golden haze
Heaven has sent to your place
I thank you God, heaven is
Here and now as I kiss
Once more, her tender brow

*Thomas Farrelly*

## EARTH

The earth spreads out her wares for everyone to see
There are so many lovely scenes for each to share
And here no pay is needed all those gifts are free
For nature only begs that we see beauty there
The sun paints all the world with gold as she goes by
And little clouds will slowly drift with quiet ease
The hills are proudly standing reaching to the sky
The gardens show their flowers dancing in the breeze
Soft fields are painted green with daisies peeping shy
The silver moon shines down to see the world asleep
Tall mountains soaring up will lift our hearts on high
Oceans keep their magic we dare not probe the deep
The Lord of all creation gave us this lovely earth
But the greatest gift of all was when He gave us birth.

*M Walker*


## A HAPPY 100TH BIRTHDAY, KELLOGG'S

Dr John Harvey Kellogg was a generous soul,
He gave us nutrition in a bowl.
He wasn't interested in money or gain,
But saving the poor from hunger and pain.
He and Will rolled out some soggy flakes,
Then put them into the oven to bake.
The resulting toasted golden flakes,
They began to make for all our sakes.
They set up the Toasted Cornflake company,
But that was only the start of the story.
For now Cocoa Pops and peanut butter,
Also make our taste buds flutter.

*G E Khandelwal*

## BLESSED ARE WE

They are full of life and energy
tiny people of our earth,
Until you hold one very dear,
you will never know their worth.
They make you laugh but also cry,
it makes you well aware,
They make you want to love them,
and show how much you care.
A sparkle in their little eyes,
a giggle loud and shrill,
the life force that they all emit,
will never fail to thrill.
A tiny hand is held aloft,
In asking for your love,
and as you love your children
Count your blessings from above.

*Linda Moore*


## DO YOU REMEMBER?

Years ago, going to he cinema
was like a great adventure!
Films were, usually, inspired by books
and not, like now, by the actors' looks!
I'll never forget 'For Whom The Bell Tolls'
where even minor characters were tops!
'Two Days and Two Nights of Love and Death'
during the Spanish Civil war:
the actors were Ingrid Bergman and Gary Cooper,
Hemingway's novel became a best seller!
Need I say that now, for me, the cinema is dead?

*Romana Bartosiak*

## DRIFTWOOD

I sit alone on the sea worn rock,
Far from the crowds, a desolate spot.
Watching the sea as it pounds the shore,
Listening to the deafening sound of the sea's roar

There is still an eerie feel to this forgotten land,
from days of old when caves were filled with contraband
Smugglers with their lanterns giving them light
guiding them to the beach under the cover of night

I lose myself in the reverie of those days afore,
picturing doomed wrecks washed up onto the shore
The bodies of the crew, bloated, floating face down
Their wives and children gathered, I hear the wailing sounds

I feel a damp, cold chill enveloping me
as the mist comes rolling off the sea
I must leave and get to the safety of my home
When a storm's a'brewing it's not safe to be alone

The weather in these parts can change in a flash
Suddenly lightning can strike and thunder will crash
The skies have already changed from a deep azure blue
as zigzags of yellow cast a translucent hue

Such a storm like this brought sailors to their deaths,
Cast into the sea where their souls come to rest
The sea can be both beautiful and cruel
When your number's up, to you it calls

I will be back again tomorrow to sit once more
to watch the beauty of this rugged shore,
Time and time again to this beach I will come,
Brought here by the past and present joining as one.

*Maggy Copeland*

# NEW YORK COMES TO CAMBRIDGE

We gathered in the Corn Exchange in that quintessential English
of towns
Left a soft, entrancing, late spring day for others to enjoy and play
Whilst we ignored the cool wind's sway . . .

Cacophony of sounds emerge whilst early stanzas shock our
untuned ears,
No sleeping of our senses as - through brash, bright tones of razzmatazz
From Wilby's score comes New York jazz

Such contrast to those dreaming towers and spires in this seat of
ancient learning
Frenetic sounds from Broadway street swirl round our bodies, minds
and feet
Speed up our pulses with the beat

The rhythmic swing of big band sound pursues crescendo at a
furious pace
Whilst virtuoso players show interpretations sweet and low
Of city life, no stops, all go

A shared excitement pulls us through the time warp of our imagination
Our thoughts leave now the world of brass as bands compete to
each surpass
A Westside tale of underclass

Familiar names perform their dance of strange, unsettling, new
symphonic tones
The music haunts and then off-stage harsh city anger pays its wage
And gunshot cracks explode in rage

But when last notes have died away, our minds return to face the here
and now
We celebrate the winning band, All England Masters of the land
We cheer as Fairey take the stand.

*Marilyn K Hambly*

# A SUMMER'S DAY

A sky's bright sun
A summer's day
A river blue
A white beach bay

Right beside this river blue
In colours drab and dull
A boat bobs slowly with the flow
The sounds are fit to lull

Houses bask in sunlit rows
Upon a quiet street
No people roam in calm content
Where many men should greet

Nearby streets are not traversed
Where men would often tread
Beside this slowly bobbing boat
A drab, dull coloured shed

Golden sands lay empty
Bobbing boat alone
No birdsong fills the summer sky
Alive no more, alone

*Gemma Guymer*

# AUTUMN

I hate the autumn, yes I do!
It's not for me. Perhaps for you?
The wind is blowing all around
The leaves are lying on the ground.
They lie in shades of brown and gold
I like the green, the shade of old.

And now the clocks will soon 'go back'
Then of the daylight there's a lack.
I should enjoy each change, I know.
Suppose it's better than the snow!

*Marjorie B Dixon*


## PHOTOGRAPH

I remember snow falling like tissue paper
nervously pulled from an unhitched sky.
The angled gate behind me.
You. Leery; poking fun;
shouting muffled words.
Now I am trying to remember
the nuance of something
said a long time ago.

I could shake you.
Grinning wisecracks; unreachable;
I don't want to reach you any more.

I just want to know how two strangers,
standing in perpetuity,
managed to smile. Live.
Arrange this nonsense.
These mute objects.
Crooked signals.
this frozen body language.

All captured perfectly, in an instant.
So I can stare, in retrospect.
Remember the loose-cried shoulders,
and realise I didn't know you at all.

*Susan Roberts*

## LIKE YESTERDAY

A day in July,
a Friday night,
unlucky for some,
but for who, me or you?
So many people, I knew who were there,
so many people now gone.
There were even a few who pretended to care,
I never thought you'd be one.
But I remember those early days
when you found love in your soul,
and I'd see trust on your face,
it makes me sad to see you now
on you these things look out of place.
Still, I can remember before you changed,
so vividly those naive days.
When we both thought we would stay the same.
Yes, I still feel those days,
like they were yesterday.

*I Aldridge*


## THE MASK

See the face behind the mask,
To seek the truth, a daunting task.
Delve deep into those lying eyes,
See deceit behind the smile.
Stop and ponder for a while.
A lifetime spent behind the mask,
Hidden from the world to see,
The you they never come to know.
Maybe yes or maybe no.

*B R B George*

# RETURN TO FANCOURT AVENUE

I don't know why I went to your old house -
The barren, roseless borders made me cry,
The fragrance of the blooms to me denied
While dandelion clocks just floated by.
Why did my steps take me to your old house?
There was no point - I knew you'd not be there
But memories sweet and sad still lingered on,
I thought I heard your voice . . . I said a prayer.
And then I saw a drift of sapphire blue
Forget-me-nots too small to dry - to frame.
I will not now go back to your old house
Without you it will never be the same.
No cheeky robin hopped along the sill.
The quietness of the house just wasn't right.
I though of how we'd laughed and danced and loved
And how we'd lain together in the night.
But all was still, so still in your old house
That once upon a time I'd thought was ours
Then from long grass a cat awoke and stretched
And took a walk on weeds where once were flowers.
When suddenly the front door opened wide
I wondered who lived there . . . my thoughts went wild.
Not wanting to be seen, behind the fence,
I hid and saw a pretty, little child
Emerge from your old house *and now it lives!*
A doll from dimpled hand was dropped on lawn.
The child laughed and Mum from the window smiled.
I dried my tears . . . *your old house was reborn.*

*Elizabeth Penn-Bennett*

## TO OUR WONDERFUL AND SPECIAL SON DAVID

From the day our arms first held you at the moment
of your birth
Little were we to know the value of your worth

Your sweet and downy head so soft, your eyes so big and blue
There we sat in tears, in awe!
Of beautiful you.

Then came school days, my how the years have flown,
you changed into a man overnight it seemed,
a mind of your very own.

You have become a son to be proud of and proud of you we are,
no matter what you do, no matter what you are,
you're still our wonderful boy the best of sons
By far.

Your mum.

*Pat Moore*


## DO NOT LEAVE ME

If you should go what would I do
Life being good to share with you,
To fill the void, relieve the pain
Past joys I'd think over again
Just full of love and care so true.

Every day my love just grew
Ever stronger only for you,
The times it seems you'd keep me sane
If you should go.

The thought of such I here eschew
Might come, the tears I'd shed not few
Would down the cheeks to leave a stain
Reveal the way I'd feel be plain
For all to see and be your due,
If you should go.

*J R Reading*


## BREATH OF LIFE

You were there when I was nothing,
Nothing on this Earth.
You were there inside of me
As from the womb I burst.
At that time I was protected,
I had little to do but learn.
As I travelled rocky pathways,
Of which there was no return.
My yearnings were many,
But rewards were very few.
Except for the one who became my wife,
And the births of our children too.
The passage of time has gone quickly,
A mere three score years and ten,
And now I feel you're leaving me
As I lie here on my bed.
Maybe when you leave me
And my time on earth is through.
We'll meet again in another world,
And together we will start anew.

*E H Timmins*

## ALL YEAR SMILE

It's always a time
When winter has gone
The summer is here
There's things to be done.

Out comes the mower
To cut down the grass
Out comes the broom
To sweep leaves off the path.

The garden needs weeding
Ready for your plants
Make sure they get water
To give them a chance.

You look at your fence
It looks a mess
Will you repair, or replace it?
It's your guess.

The windows need painting
So does the door
Your gutter is hanging
Down on the floor.

The days are lighter
For longer in the day
But there's load of jobs
To be done anyway.

Is winter that bad?
When it is here
Cheer yourself up
And smile all the year.

*Rob Passmore*

## SHIMMERING STAR

Iridescent hue
Rainbow shades
Of blue, green and purple
Shimmer
Reflecting the morning sunlight
Shining
Like a jewel
Sapphire, emerald, amethyst
Precious
Perfection
Perching on a flower spike
Giving his all
Singing
Displaying
With the sea as his backdrop
Just take time
He's worth a second glance
This so familiar comic character
Once common
Sadly now declining
What could it be?
Our versatile
Much maligned
Beautiful
Starling

*J Stanley*

## THE LITTLE BEGGAR BOY

A little boy begging, alone, in despair
Hungry in the heat of a dusty dirty street
I will never forget that pathetic pleading stare

He is too innocent to accuse those who do not care
And people who give and walk away feel guilty to leave
A little boy begging, alone, in despair

In so many countries I have seen him there
Hand held out, hoping you will not pass him by
I will never forget that pathetic pleading stare

I do not know who he is but I feel aware
That somehow we are all to blame for the plight of
A little boy begging, alone, in despair

He will always be somewhere in need of care
I do not see him now but I know he is there
A little boy begging, alone, in despair
I will never forget that pathetic pleading stare

*Kenneth Benoy*


## DO NOT WISH YOUR LIFE AWAY

Do not wish your life away,
Just live it day by day,
God gives you love and peace and health
And happiness while you may.

Do not wish your life away
Spread happiness where you can
There's lots to do and lots to see
It's all part of the plan.

Do not wish your life away
But think of all the pleasure
That you can bring to other folk
And do it at your leisure.

From sin and hate you must adhere
From jealousy and spite
For happy people live happy lives
And so they reach the heights.

*Pamela J New*

## A FISHY TAIL - TALE

The world is like a goldfish bowl
Floating round in space.
And we're just one of many *prawns*
Competing in a race.
Some of us are just little *sprats*
And some of us are big large *pike*
And some of us maybe big *white sharks*
That not many people like.

But it really doesn't matter,
How big or small we are.
Whether we ride around on pushbikes
Or drive a big flash car.
The world is our *oyster*
It's there for everyone.

So don't *clam* up.
*Splash* out a while
And have yourself some fun.

*Charles Pelham*

# CAUS

*(A village in Shropshire, deserted and abandoned in the 14th Century)*

The field-wobble registers the seismic rain.

Rotting wood wisdom teeth poke the green floorboards, whilst
Her aerial tortoise shell sward is a dead giveaway.
One of three thousand, she shrouds her muddy bones with firs,
Only her strips are felt by the camera.

Abandoned records and revenues moulder black
With the coulters left Dutchman-like in the furrows.
A wreath of soil in Langland's inky palm,
Vill and assarts rumble under the tractor.

The Corve's smallpox scars, Upper Severn's hives
Are very slow healers;
Bandaged by enclosures,
Wedged by Silurian splints
Is the Norman stitched incision.

Sunken ridges on the foreheads
Of her poor dependants
Were etched by sweat and flies.
Long washed bridges over ditches
Of God-fearing tenants
Were fossilised before their eyes.

Flaying your small skin for flints,
They trowel your flesh by air,
Exposing the landowner,
Evicting the priest,
Earning honours degrees with care.

Hollow-ways and cart racks
Were ground by a mill of hooves:
Eraser of gravel,
Spade-flattened loam,
New X-rayed from above the rooves.

Nothing to do with nothing,
The Teme and the Tern still flow
Out of Caus's dried up veins
Into the Severn's bone-filled drain:
Saxon skeletons on the open sea row.

A pock-mark on England
That had its thronging towers,
Now swabbed by clod cotton wool,
Streaked traces of king, serf and fool
From the pasture of millions of hours.

*A Strange*


## SONGBIRDS GALORE

so sweet the voice of the wild songbird
no sweeter a voice have I ever heard
and no nicer a tune have I ever found
such a peaceful and captivating sound

oh how I love to hear the wild birds sing
as I stroll through woodland in the spring
I stop awhile and I listen to their call
yes how I love to hear them one and all

the song of the chaffinch and the robin too
the thrush and the blackbird to name just a few
there are many more whose titles I cannot recall
as I listen to their tunes in the trees so tall

just to hear the dawn chorus when I first awake
at very first light as a new day does break
it is such an enchanting and wondrous sound to hear
the tunes of the wild birds that we cherish so dear

*A V Carlin*

## WHAT CHRISTMAS MEANS TO ME

Christmas time when I was small
Was all about Santa coming to call
The excitement of listening on that sleepless night
For Santa to come down the chimney, oh so tight
During teenage years it was all about
Meeting with friends and going out
And in the years when love was new
It was a quiet Christmas just for two.

But in time the family came along
And Christmas played a different song
With playgroup Christmas party fun
A loaf of sandwiches must be done
And lots of presents to wrap and tie
All ready for Santa when he comes by
It was worth it just to see the joy
On the face of every girl and boy.

Then came the schools' concerts and plays
I've celebrated Christmas in so many ways
But always at its heart there's been
The memory of the stable scene
And Jesus' birth on that cold starry night
When he came to help make everything right
So however we celebrate let's always remember
That most magical birth on a night in December.

*Linda Perry*

# WOODLAND WONDERS

*(Dedicated to Carole Mills for helping me when I came out of hospital.
I would not have coped without you - thanks)*

See the sunlight dappling thru
Leaves of trees, in sky so blue.
As sun sets the sky's a-flame.
Woodland wonders is the game.

Hark! A'trampling in the copse.
Majestic stag stands still, hops
When startled and clears a gate.
Wondrous in might, where's his mate?

Moonlight silvers woodland bright
In the darkness of the night.
Inky bathed, then bright with light.
Truly it's a lovely sight.

Barn owl screeches high on wing.
Not seen, just imagining
A streak of white/golden shine.
After prey for foods in line.

Primroses arrive in spring,
Bluebells then do ring-a-ling.
In the pond the tadpoles hatch
Bringing on the froggie batch.

Fronds of ferns uncoil to stay
Fluffy-like, many a day.
Heather purple in the wood
*Woodland wonders very good.*

**Margaret E Preston**

## BARR - BEACON - GREAT BARR: 1940's

When we were young, my brother and I
would take our dog Paddy
to Barr Beacon, and there we'd stay.
While away the summer hours
admit the heather, gorse and flowers
underneath the summer sky
. my brother Graham and I.
Only a short walk, from our home
green fields, hills and stream.
All day we'd stay, play and dream
as years went by, teenagers we became.
Our first sweetheart, our first kiss
on Barr Beacon, it was bliss!
There we would stroll hand-in-hand
on Sunday, after lunch.
Then home for tea, it was grand.
A big map, underneath the dome
on Barr-Beacon, miles and miles shown.
In war-time a huge gun Big Bertha
on Barr Beacon stood, the noise shook and shook.
The years have flown, Paddy our dog is gone,
but how those memories linger on.
Whatever happened to that first beau
I guess he's just a memory now.
We'll never know!
Happy days of long ago, stirred
by a photo from the past.
Memories of Barr-Beacon, youth
winter snow of 46-47, sledges, fun, laughter
of happiness that forever will last.

*Irene G Corbett*

## MAUREEN'S OLD CHINA SHOP

The colours she uses are expressive and bright;
Primrose, green, blue and white.
The brush strokes cover many things, some
we take for granted, like birds on the wing.
As she spins the wheel, and does her share,
the noise around is hard to bear.
Constant chatter, the flow of ware, the smell
of spirits, the lack of air.
An endless task, a very long day, to make a
living, to pay her way.
The end result is a work of art, painted
with feeling, right from the heart.
Each piece of pot, simply unique,
finished by hand, and the brush
so to speak . . .

*I Welch*


## CLEETHORPES
*(Or Any Seaside In Winter)*

The saddest place is the seaside
when the summer's gone away.
And the promenade is haunted
by children at play.
The fun-fair now quite lonely
with no one there to ride.
And the gulls sound so eerie
on the incoming tide.
It's all very strange, waiting for
the fun to start.
But it's just the place for a
broken heart.

*J Johnson*

## EPITAPH

Shingle fringe of quiet sandy beach.
Two wooden crosses stand
with everlasting flowers
over two pebbled graves.

Last year, a story in the local paper:
experienced fisherman takes teenage nephew
night-fishing where the currents run,
not dressed for dirty weather,
no life jackets . . .

Two wooden crosses stand
over two pebbled graves.
One says: *John Emlyn RIP* with date;
the other simply . . .
*Dad.*

**G Nussbaum**


## THIS ENGLAND

Drive slowly down this lane, cow-parsley, knee high
Will froth a lacy wake long after you go by,
And wayside hedges creamed with flowers
Will scent the air, while warm spring showers
Spread growing corn in a surge of green
On furrowed fields that the hawthorns screen.

Walk slowly through this field, buttercups, bright gold
Will shimmer sunlit radiance a thousand fold;
Not till next year the housing estate,
Now children play by the swinging gate.
Do you like butter? The age old game,
Could this one English field stay always the same!

**Sheila Town**

# A LOVELY EVENING IN CRICCIETH

The evening sun casts a warm shroud of light
                                                over the clear coastline.
Seemingly making it closer than before.
Shadows are thrown as far as the fisherman's line.
The white fluffy clouds sit on top of the mountains,
                                                the dark sky is no more.

Then with horror a young girl shrieks.
She thinks she has noticed a shark in the sea.
This bay isn't what the sharks do seek.
It's the friendly dolphin just swum in for his tea.

Gradually as the night closes in and the full moon
                                                shows herself in the sky.
She cascades a tunnel of light from the horizon to
                                                the beach.
Only occasionally does the cascade blot out by
                                                small clouds drifting by.
And the lights from the towns shimmers as if
                                                within easy reach.

Couples chatter as they wander along the
                                                Marine Drive.
Enjoying their walk and breathing the air.
It may be their last stroll by the sea and
                                                a time for a dive.
A shop is still open to take back Welsh fare.

*M Baxter*

## THE SINGER

I heard you singing in my dream
awakening I find your voice
unravelling my seams
making sense of nonsense
making love like a songbird.

I recognise you when we aren't there
in a space created by a mind that's fired
hot-wired but unwinding
slowing down the beating
of a heart that's tired.

You show me how soothing
it can be, to sing . . .

So I follow the song that is sung
and bask in the sunshine and warmth,
the smile on my face
is but the smallest trace
of the selfless love that you gave.

So I came looking for you in the space
somewhere between wake and rest.
Your voice the flutter of wing
on the wind reminds me again
of the song that you sing.

You show me how soothing
it can be, to dream . . .

*C Jackson*

# MEMORIES

Life's memories surround us,
They build up day by day;
Some are best forgotten
While the happiest ones will stay.

The solitary notes of birdsong
In the early hours of dawn -
When sleep is far, so far away
Before the break of morn.

The warm hand of a small child
With hair like burnished gold
And eyes so soft and trusting
Make a picture to behold.

The long grass in an orchard
Where happy children play;
The days and days of sunshine
Seem endless - miles away.

The sweetest scent of flowers
On a perfect summer's day,
When in the cool of evening
The insects dance and play.

The happy smiling faces
Of loved ones now at rest
Will linger on forever,
The dearest and the best.

A place for each and every one
And many more besides,
Which nothing else will quite replace
Beyond the realms of time.

*Joan Mathers*

## RAINBOWS

A rainbow in the sky
Makes us wonder why
Rain and sun together
Give unusual weather.
Yellow, red, green and blue,
With touch of orange too;
Although it curves and bends
It seems to have no ends.
One moment it is there,
Then it will disappear.
It's God's sign that we should
Not have another flood.
For his next show of ire
Will set the world on fire.

*Doris E Briggs*


## ELDERLY REFUGEE FINDS FOOD ON THE ROAD FROM KOSOVO

So grimly griped the granny,
Gorged and gasped and grumbled
As she gulped her gloomy gutful;

Ghastly was her glower,
Shrivelled her flower,
Forgone her power.

Cock-robin by the blossom
Spun his jolly song of woe
For empty crop and gizzard
And hungry mate and nestlings -
Warm starvation days of spring!

*A Cohen*

# PEACOCK

I shall never forget my first peacock.
We were at Kew - I was two,
and perhaps three months.
For I was born in March and the rhododendrons
were in bloom. Mother
was sitting, looking at something
she had brought with her. I, on tip-toe to plunge my face
in every magenta, every purple, every rose-pink, every
shell-pink, every crimson flower, moved around
the bed of bushes, and so found
I stood in a different dell.
From the other corner entered the most amazing
woman I had ever seen; short, dressed all
in brilliant, flashing blue. Black balls
upon her hat-pins stood straight up
and wobbled as she walked.
Her cheeks were the most ghastly white,
her eyes black points, level with mine,
as was her jabbing nose or beak.
Woman or monstrous bird! I knew my danger
and stood absolutely still.
The dreadful face deflected to one side.
The huge shoulders, in their shimmering shawl passed
and with a slowness that seemed to take an age
the endless train of eyed and iridescent feathers passed.

I felt it as a punishment
for having got out of sight of Mother.
And when I slipped back to her
did not tell her of this adventure.

*Jean Overton Fuller*

## WHY?

She was smart, attractive and supreme
Her name - Evelyn Greene
A love of life, of sun and rain
Baking soda bread and apple pie
Until one day she felt a pain
Her eyes turned to Heaven in the sky
She lost her sparkle and her hair
and cried out in despair
'Why Lord? Why me?'
Unlock my grief with God's own key.

The Rector came, with honest prayers
The hospital bed awash with tears
The doctor announced *three weeks to live*
No reprieve, just sadness to give
Two years ago this was said
and still Evelyn Greene lies in bed
She prays each day for God to take her
Away from suffering and pain
To Heaven and the cancer slain.

*Dennis R Rowe*


## COMPANIONS

I've always loved being with you
I am warm and snug in your care
I know I have irritated you in the past
I was hoping we could be a pair.

You have tried your best to get rid of me
But I'm not so easily led
When you are asleep at night
I often creep into your bed.

Your mother thinks I'm a *nit*
But I don't really care
I'm content and happy where I am
I'm just the *louse* in your hair.

*Mabel Utting*


## THE DAM

The November day is dark and sombre.
The sky is black tinged with purple like a funeral pall.
A curtain of hail and sleet like bullets fall from the sky.
There stands the dam, huge, stark almost menacing.
High into the air it reaches, twin towers at each end, like sentries stand.
The reservoir behind is large, deep, and still with menacing power
Through the sluices the waters froth and fume.
They tumble into the ground below, to do what they must.
I walk along the causeway straight and the walls hide me.
The end leads into a rocky and treacherous path.
It clings to the side of the cliff and continues up into the hills.
I turn and look back and see the dam in all its solemnity.
Fear creeps into my heart and soul, with awful dread.
The dam guards and keeps, and holds the waters tight.
Yet the water is great, a mighty force, and could destroy.
If the walls were breached, all hell would be let loose.
Farms would vanish, animals would perish, all remaining
                                          is water, water,
The dam is strong and holds the waters tight and will not give
                                          in without a fight.
I leave this place, and descend to the twinkling lights below.
I reach the cottage warm and bright, open the door and see the
                                          fire burning bright.
I am home at last, safe as I can be.

*Carl Kemper*

# MAN'S DESTRUCTIVE HAND

Must we first kill to know that it's wrong?
Must we destroy until everything has gone?
Why does man keep having to say
this is my world, I'll do things my way?
But it isn't just his world, it isn't his choice.
He believes it's his because he has a voice.
'What of the people, plants and animals I destroy,
the earth is for man to use as his toy.'
Seal pups are killed pointlessly
just to ensure there is more fish in the sea.
Man killed the Dodo, it can't be brought back.
Endangered whales are killed to make soap from their fat.
The rainforests are being destroyed, yet they may hold the key
to curing many diseases, but man still cannot see.
Animals are being driven from their natural habitat,
into captivity for we find only that,
can save these animals from progressive man,
as he continues to destroy in a way only he can.
Soon all the wild animals and plants will be no more,
leaving man alone in a world to abhor,
at the destruction he mindlessly created.
A destruction that many had anticipated.
But their words had fallen on deaf ears,
for now was the realisation of their greatest fears.
A world void of life except that of man,
in a world fashioned by his destructive hand.

*D C N Johnson*

## HARLESTONE BEECHES

Have you noticed when I pass
O'er this year last
When I walk within the glade
In your shadow and your shade
Four seasons now have term run
From winter's cold to summer sun
Of the pleasures I would list
A walk in winter embraced in mist
That heightens the sense
Of others lost to recompense
With the only sound within the trees
Is the drip of water onto fallen leaves
But if I let my attention stray
Well-formed buds now hold my gaze
Within the husks they hold
The future this spring to be told.

*B Norman*


## NIGHT FALL

Gold and purple glows the sky
As evening time draws near
And clouds that scud away up high
Leave all around so clear
The moon arises full of grace
With light to show the way
And birds go to their resting place
Till dark turns into day
The sun arises way up high
Just like her sister moon
Bringing to each a deep blue sky
And life is all in tune.

*Sheila Elkins*

## DOUBTS AND FEARS

I dare not think what lies ahead,
I've made my choice now must be led,
by fate.
But how alone I feel
this foggy day so damp and drear.

Vague shapes loom from this hanging net
like spectres with their arms outstretched.
I must step onwards steadfastly.
Ignore the ghosts still haunting me.

These shadows from my life thus far
mirror the mist, obscure my path.
What lies ahead is yet unseen,
The route I've trod has vanished, gone.

I'll journey on where fate will lead,
the fog will lift, the sun will ease
the chill, damp darkness gripping me.
The view ahead may then be seen.

*Juliette Blencowe*


## SUICIDAL THOUGHTS

So I guess the feeling's back
Under the skin my heart bleeds black
I thought I'd lost it long ago
Caused by something I will never know
In the water I went under
Drowning I began to wonder
All the time thinking one more breath
Lying to myself as I thought about death.

The depression starting coming again
How long will it be before I feel the pain
On an empty bed I lay
Under the covers I'm locked away
Going nowhere but running fast
Hurrying to get there but I'm always last
Tighter the noose will never slack
Suicidal thoughts are back.

*Joanne Spencer*

## KILLING TIME

Went to the pub the other night,
got into a terrible fight,
kicking in heads, knocking down doors,
smashing up tables, painting the floors.

I'm just killing time.
I said killing time,
Killing
Killing time
I'm just killing time . . .

Woke up battered and bruised, my ma,
said you're born to lose.

I'm just killing time.
I said killing time.

I met a girl and got married,
wot the hell, I'm just killing time.

*Paul Walton*

# OLD JACK

While out walking, Eli stopped for a while
and saw a sight that made him smile.
Old Jack was on the top of his house
holding a small tree.
It looked precarious for a man
well over seventy-three.
'What doing Jack?' he called getting
quite hot.
As Jack stood leaning against
the chimney pot.
'I'm shoving the tree down the chimney,
to get rid of the soot.
I'm safe enough' he said 'I've a piece of rope
tied around my foot.'
'Why don't you let your sons do it?'
Eli said, 'and save all this worry.'
'I can't wait for them, Jack said
I'm in a bit of a hurry.'
Eli said his farewells, and went
on his way.
Seeing old Jack performing
had brightened his day.
Old Jack never wanted status in
life or wealth.
It was more important to him to
stay in good health.

Jack was my father, and never showed
fear.
And in my heart, I hold him so dear.

***Margaret Clowes***

## THREE FRIENDS ON HOLIDAY

The sea, the sand
the high jagged cliff.
If only we could stay,
If only, if . . .

The green rolling hills
where we love to walk.
Our laughs, our giggles.
How we love to talk.

We're past our youth,
we know this is true.
But we feel so young.
When sea and sky are blue.

If time would standstill
or just slow down.
To stay here in peace.
Away from the town.

To just lie here
and doze and nap.
If only we could stay.
And not go back.

We'll miss this view
of sun, sand and sea.
But we will come back.
Carol, Pam and me . . .

*Christine Sharp*

## WORCESTER IN THE SPRINGTIME

Oft upon a lifetime
You may go along that way.
Into the lovely springtime
On a bright fine day.

It was a bit of heaven,
Just before the May.
The hyacinths along the wall
Were in their best array.

The tulips were rushing on
To have a second place.
But a special pot of daffodils
Had such a lovely face.

They were as fresh as April
Just standing straight and clear.
They looked you in the eye, till
You said 'You're the best this year.'

Worcester in the springtime
Down the Broadway fine.
All was quite exquisite
You must not miss a visit.

*Mildred T Kendrew*


## LOSS

Four years since we talked,
At times, I'm distraught,
I miss you.

Flowers I take,
Fond memories awake.
I love you.

You gave me your all,
Death brings a wall:

But we are still one
Your memory lives on.
I am you.

*Elizabeth Rice*


## RIP TO JOHN BETJEMAN

Milton Keynes where there is a concrete cow
No room for real ones anyhow
What would John Betjeman make of it now
I'm sure he would think it's worse than Slough
No friendly bombs to fall just now
There are long straight roads that are congested
with the motor car infested
Where there was once a lovely tree
Now stands a supermarket one two three
There is no work for men to do
They shuffle along in the dole queue
I'd send a letter but that's not vogue
There are other things that are in mode
Such as a fax, on how to dodge your Income Tax
Or surf the net get no reply
the screen's gone dead I don't know why
I'll get on my mobile phone and press recall
To tell you life's not changed at all
My heart it longs for days gone by
A quieter more peaceful life for I
But I'm afraid it is not to be
We are in the age of technology
now entering the millennium you see.

*Mary Buttle*

## SHE WILL RETURN NOT AGAIN

The girl I knew very well,
my head she made swim.
Our love did swell,
but now the story is grim.

Gone is she by the grace of God,
to a better place than mine.
Chosen by the divine rod,
whose power I cannot define.

I loved her, so why take her?
I would have taken care here.
What God would you prefer,
lost lovers left in a glare.

Think well and please explain,
miss not a single crumb.
Consider the loss and pain,
your answer must be a plum.

Who am I, you may ask,
Who questions you now?
Daring to take you to task,
perhaps cause a row.

Give her back you will not,
but her memory you cannot take.
On this earth I may rot,
but from love I will not quake.

Ah, I hear you say,
his weakness now shows.
He will go away and pray,
and seeds for sympathy he sows.

No Lord that is not so.
Don't you see
my love to heaven does go,
for my girl and for me.

Having now thought about my loss
and the gain made above.
There is not a coin to toss,
just the flight of a dove.

*K J Humphrey*


## SOUL MATES

Your head against my shoulder rests
my chest against your breasts
our arms around each other
making sure we do not smother
you I find within my mind
restoring my soul
I stroke your face
such beauty such grace
you move in our warm embrace
your eyes open wide
then close again
absorbing me deep inside
wherein I find
within your mind
forgiveness lovingness eternalness
oh mistress mine so divine
let our minds spirits bodies entwine
in total harmony
throughout eternity.

*W B McDade*

## MODERN LIFE

Rats running in the gutters, debris everywhere,
People rushing to and fro their noses in the air.
Looking with averted eyes
Not wanting to see what they despise.

Graffiti, decay. No more children at play.
Litter and smell, that makes one repel
Making the bile rise
Bringing tears to the eyes.

Building's empty, windows and doors smashed in,
Remnants of wallpaper, once there was life within.
What is life an empty shell
A pile of bricks, left where they fell.

Walking along empty streets, staring back with a look so bleak,
Once houses stood with fronts so neat,
Why have so many brought you down, a great pity!
Once we could boast a beautiful city!

*Blanche Middleton*


## THE CHANGING YEARS

To see beauty and hold it in my hands to feel,
then you know that beauty in life is real.
And time passes by like a shadow,
and age flies like a sleek swallow.

But my mind gets slower with age,
like my fingers turning over a page.
And each step taken is like walking uphill,
But the sweet scent of nature, I still get my fill.

And of youth I dream and still remember,
the gift of life is like a dying ember.
But like the grains of sands, do shift.
The years of my life and age do upwards lift.

*M L Fletcher*


## HISTORY IN THE SKY

Dark and sombre
She stood on the ground
Engines still
Not a sound
With wings spanning wide
The Lancaster bomber
A symbol of pride
Men once flew in her
Fearless and brave
For king and country
Young lives they gave
Suddenly into life
Her engines roared
Speeding down the runway
Like a bird she soared
Flying majestically on high
Now visiting airshows
History in the sky
Jets now stand
On airfields of old
Flown by airmen
Skilled and bold
Breaking the sound barrier
Screaming through the sky
New technology
New ways to fly.

*Brenda M Hadley*

## THE SOCIAL CLIMATE

The social climate
And the social climbers who climb it.
A nouveau *niche* for the nouveau *riche*.
Central figures in the microfiche
Of the bistro beach.
The misfits of fortune,
Not really rich, not really poor.
Halfway house proud with new antique door.

The *haves* have what the *have-nots* have not,
They're the *have-ishs*, radishes betwixt
The peas and the pounds.
The cod piece between the piece of steak
And the potato cake
On the Balmoral barbecue skewer.
Halfway down the pecking order
Between the culture vultures
And the pidgin English.

*Keith Loines*


## TODAY I SAW YOU MY LOVE

Just two months ago you died,
and since that day, I've cried and cried.
I miss you, and I always will,
though you've gone, you're still my Bill.

Today once more I heard you speak,
and at the sound my knees went weak.
I saw you walk across the room,
as you whistled that old familiar tune.

You turned to me with that winning smile,
and you felt close for just a while.
Your eyes they sparkled like the dew,
as you whispered softly 'I love you.'

I sat in my chair and shed a tear
as I watched you disappear.
I slowly got up as in a dream,
and removed the tape from my video machine.

*Pauline Wilkins*


## FOND THOUGHTS ON PHOTOGRAPHING A GIRL BY A SUNDIAL

Have you e'er thought that in some moment fleeting
    Experiencing some great beauty or rare joy,
That you could stay the sands of time from falling,
    Their unrelenting task not to employ.

That you could make those precious moments linger
    And not like dreams too quickly fade away,
    By turning one brief minute to an hour,
    And then stretch one whole hour into a day.

But though we wish in vain of time to borrow,
    He will not stay but to eternity -
Makes joys today just memories for tomorrow,
    Dissolving into mists of antiquity.

So we must seek by other means and cunning,
    Those moments of life's pleasures to renew;
    And as beside his monument you linger,
    I've caught this moment ever more for you.

*Godfrey Nall*

## SCOTLAND'S MAGIC

Rocky, majestic mountains so high,
pierce the pale blue morning sky.
Climbing, surrounding, tall and strong,
evergreen fir trees rooted there belong.
As silent soldiers, waiting and
guarding.
From mountain tops pure white snow
is melting,
Cold sparkling water, soon is gushing
Sliding downwards, speedily rushing,
Weaving its way onwards, quickly knowing
To the little springs it must be going.
Faster and faster through green fields
flowing
Rolling over pebbles, jumping stones,
trickling
Happily along under wooden bridges
travelling.
Transporting needy water to all living,
Sheep, cattle, birds and humans
thirsting!
The early morning mysterious Scottish
mist,
The purple Highland heather, gently
kissed.
The hedgerows and flowers give off
their scent,
Lucky campers, snugged up, asleep in
their tent.
Rainfalls in Scotland's Highlands -
don't I know,
Yet it's a truly magical place to go!

*Stella Bush-Payne*

## THE SEALIFE

take that smile right off your face
said the haddock to the plaice
the kipper thought he looked a prat
not unlike his friend the sprat
the oyster always prone to brag
often boasting to the crab
the little squid felt not too well
and gave off quite a nasty smell
the jumpy shark had brushed its teeth
and went out hunting in the reef
the shocking eel was feeling low
and thought the sea snail moved too slow
all God's sealife sharing space
careful not to spoil the place

*D Carter*


## EARLY MORNING

This morning, something woke me up,
I don't know what for!
Then I heard a chirrup, a whistle, then a caw,
It was that marvellous chorus that
Each morning fills the air,
With bluetits, robins, sparrows, flying everywhere.
What joy there is in a silence,
That lets nature sing so strong!
Before the noise and bustle of a day coming on,
What tone, what sounds, what notes?
Sweet music to a mind that floats,
Through sleep and wake, joy, dismay,
Last week, tomorrow, another day!

*Carol Mac*

# A LANCASHIRE DREAM

Outside a factory gate in Lancashire,
I saw a sight extremely queer,
A crowd of elongated people, with elongated legs,
And attached to their bodies were elongated heads.

I had never seen such a sight before.
The policeman on his beat was seven feet tall.
He had boots like longboats on his feet,
Which went clickety-clack as he walked down the street.

A matchstick girl was playing with a hoop,
Being six feet tall she had to stoop.
This action caused her a deal of trouble
For the matchstick girl had to bend over double.

Suddenly my mother was shaking me.
'Wake up lad, have a cup of tea.'
Then I realised I was having a dream,
to which one of Lowry's pictures had
set the scene.

### *E Holmes*


# UNTITLED
*(Based on taking a walk just after Christmas in January,
wandering for miles trying to get my ex-wife out of my head.)*

Battered and bruised, one of life's ill-used
Upon snowcapped mountains I gaze.
Tranquillity reigns with peace of mind
As a watery sun endeavours to shine.

Ice frozen lakes, life's picture it makes
The acres all covered with snow.
The long winding road and the valleys below
Nature's canvas to man, take for granted we know.

The grey mist descends as the daylight ends
North winds they gather to blow.
Quiet is the night and so still is life
Throughout our beautiful moor lands glow.

*Martin Gabriel Kane*


## A TRIBUTE

If I had a mother
I would handle her with care
I would love her forever
So I never need despair
That ever-loving feeling
The smile that greets you there
When you feel down she'll pick you up
And chase away your gloom.

If you have a mother
Treat her with special care.
For into this world she bore you
With loving tender care
She'll be there if ever needed
And wipe away your tears
She'll put you right when you go wrong
And help you through the years.

For when life's knocks get you down
There is no need to sit and frown
For she will sit and she will share
All your worries, with great care
So if you have your mother
Treasure her with pride
For there's no greater friend
Than a mother to life's end.

*Brenda Brownhill*

## HEAT

Seared by thoughts
Never spoken.
The tide of time
Retreats from the baking sand
Where oiled bodies
Lie like sizzling sausages,
Ripe with succulent juices.
There on my raft
I find myself once more
Drifting further
And further;
Being carried away
Helplessly
From the fleshy shore;
Trying desperately to return
With cupped hands
Thrashing insanely
In the cool, clear water.

*Paul Howard*


## FORBIDDEN LOVE

I have swam the moon's silver light;
Danced with stars amongst the night
I held the sun of eternal flame;
And with my heart; I wrote your name.

I have sang with birds; The chorus of dawn;
So thrilled I sang my love was born
I flew with bees; Around scented flowers;
In the presence of love; I was lost for hours.

I heard the chimes off bluebells petals;
Beware the love; With poison nettles
But my eyes were blind so blind to see;
Your love was chained and wanted free.

So I stood by the river; At water's edge'
And felt the pain begin to wedge
For love was a season; A season, but a day;
Your unchained love; Had flown away.

*David Johnathan Daniels*


## THE STAR

A star so bright, a star so small, yet so brilliant,
Shone the night that Christ was born, in a stable.
No mansion or a warm home for this child.
Born in humility.
Surrounded by Mary, God's chosen mother for His son,
And Joseph, a carpenter, his earthly father.
They were the guests of the animals whose stable they shared.

They were ordinary people, the kind Christ was to
Walk amongst, to teach, to heal, to preach, on many
Occasions in story form, in a language that simple
People understand.
He was born to be our Saviour.
Yet from birth his parents had to flee from Bethlehem
Because of Herod, who sought to kill him.
Throughout his life of merely thirty-three years, he was to be rejected.
They failed to recognise the beauty of the Son of God.

Will you keep open the door to your heart?
Will there be no room at the inn, for the Christ child,
When this Christmas is passed.
He is the most brilliant star that ever came to earth.
Hallowed is His name.

*Maureen Margaret Huber*

## SILENCE?

There is no such thing as silence.
Silence does not exist. Some may say this room is silent,
*But* my ears are caught up in a web of motion
Tangled by sounds
Unheard
Silence. Silence?
The battle between big clock and small.
The alternate ticking on alternate wall.
High-pitched and rapid
Low-pitched and slow,
Each catching the other in mid-tick, mid-tock.
Unheard.
Silence. Silence?
A whine of wheels passes the window,
Passing from slowly, through quick, back to slow.
Grating from low-key, through high, back to low.
Unheard.
Silence. Silence?
The sound of the human
Inhaling air
Throat gulping moisture
Crunch in the ear.
Clash with the clocks,
Conflict with the cars,
Vibrating
Expanding
*Louder, louder, louder!*
Silence. Silence!

*Patricia Bullock*

## THE FORGOTTEN ARMY (CHINDITS)

There is a regiment whose name all do not know,
Its sacrifices, victories are but memories now.
Their names live on in the hearts of others, so few,
The shadows of the past still vivid, still new.
They lie, these half forgotten heroes far away.
In jungle graves where nature only holds her sway.
Where silence reigns in peace, in rest,
Men who gave their everything in that one vital test.
They fought and died like heroes,
Some died and knew not why.
Others in a blaze of glory
And a few with plaintive cry.
But though they fought a battle so very far away,
Their gallantry is no less diminished to this day.
They fought as thousands more did fight and die,
For a world of peace, freedom and joy.
Their sacrifice was made that others might live on,
These husbands, brothers, young mother's son.
They questioned not that they should give,
Their precious lives that others might live.
The shadows of their glory march past in silent might.
Their names in glory shine radiantly bright.
The bugle calls for rally to these heroes who are gone.
Their voices seem to answer 'neath the crimson setting sun.
The darkness of the jungle night upon their graves has set.
Let us honour them, these heroes - lest we forget . . .

*B Ruffles*

# A HOLIDAY AT BLACKPOOL

It was centenary year at Blackpool and they had painted the
tower in pure gold,
They had built a huge rollercoaster, the world's biggest and
highest all told,
We went for a holiday that very same year and went to the top
of the tower without fear,

We got a very nice room at Pontin's, we were extremely lucky
that way,
The meals were a treat, always plenty to eat, we did have a very
nice stay,
The entertainment was arranged to suit every taste.
When it's 'Old Tyme Music Hall' there was no time to waste.
We did get a seat near some very nice folk,
When we heard where they came from, we thought it a joke!
As they were from Blackpool, and came five times a year,
They said, people do think it's funny, but it's value for money,
And we do so enjoy our time here.

I decided to enter the talent contest,
To read one of my poems, which is what I do best,
As it was the 50th anniversary of the famous D Day,
I thought the one about 'Joining the Waafs' would be really OK.
So I went on the stage with a feeling of awe,
After all, I'd never done anything quite like it before.
So I said to myself, come on, sock it to them Dot!
They're not going to shoot you, so give it all you've got.
My first time on a proper stage wasn't all that bad,
It's the kind of courage I didn't know I had.

Blackpool has three good piers of which it can boast,
And the famous tramway for eleven and a half miles along
                                                    the coast,
But the sea is so dirty I'm sorry to say.
But they are hoping to make it sparkling clean - one fine day?
The illuminations in the autumn are a joy to behold,
They bring lots of pleasure to both young and old.

*Dorothy Kells Mezaks*


# THE CHURCH

Standing alone in this holy place - bewildering - solemn to me
Words fail, they cease to be.
I need to speak, to pray, to offer something.
I raise my eyes before thee
Feeling insecure. Are you really watching me?
How can I be sure?
Your figurine, a statue, a little warmth of face.
Do I really know you? I who fell from grace.
Nervously I back away. Should I walk away - or run?
Peering over my shoulder, I see the church doors wide open
the outside world just waiting . . .
Waiting for what? Waiting for me? Silence abounds.
A tugging each way of my mind and physical body.
I'm here for a purpose, of what I'm unsure.
I *must* face my creator, though he may silence me as before.
Open up my heart of stone. I plead to thee *myself.*
Do not disgrace, more than has been done by you
I turn my head away from the doors,
and raise mine eyes up to yours.
The stone shatters in pieces -
as the tears and my love are laden on you.

*Sylvia Westwood*

## HEY-UP COZ!

Down 'the Dumps,' turn up the brickyard, steps retraced,
                                        recall, get up to date.
Nostalgic saunter, check changed vistas, new development abounds.
Country lane now busy highway, nine acres meadow housing estate,
As on foreign fields I venture. Gone Horse & Groom and Fox &
                                        Hounds.
'Progress' we know, can't be halted.
Posh new houses can't be faulted.
Shopping better? Larger store.
Local airport, good for jetting.
Cafes new, appetites wetting.
Not all bad, much to adore.

Gone the gasworks, railway station. Trains to London, perhaps to Trent.
A new restaurant that was our butcher's, fish shop that once sold socks,
Where I was born, with my sister. Road where tommies marched,
                                        Churchills went.
St Andrews stands proud, unaltered? No more winding for its clocks.
Cap & Stocking, Red Lion, New Inn.
Baptist, Methodist, Wesleyan,
Great institutions still serve
Kegworthians, all faiths, all creeds.
Give spiritual or social needs,
These both sacred to preserve.

Thus I count, recall the faces that once smiled, said 'Hey-up Coz,'
Sadly few are known by face now. Sixty years has thinned us out.
Some moved to suit their work place, their roots pulled up, some
                                                    wrench that was,
others sadly at rest early, still looking down to check, no doubt,
On how young villagers behave.
Preserve cultures their forebears gave.
For those, for me, now few,
Find precious vistas are no longer,
Yet sacred memories stay stronger,
May God protect this Kegworth new!

*Derek E Akers*


## FOREVER YOUNG

She is the eternal child
refusing to grow old -
age has not dimmed those laughing eyes,
no grey strand mars the gold.
A love of life lights up her face -
her step is firm and sprightly -
adventure still she seeks to find -
time sits upon her lightly.
She will not submit to earnest pleas
that it is time to join the clan
of those who now sit at their ease -
that never was her plan!
The fires of youth still blaze within
there is yet much to be done -
and whilst her love for life goes on
she will stay forever young.

*Connie Smith*

## Fantasy Journey

I walked through a field where the trees were all people,
In the middle of the field was no church but a steeple.
Blue frogs were leaping everywhere,
They all had very long purple hair.
There sat a cat with a mighty grin,
With a notice above which read do come in.
I scurried on past as fast as I could,
And came to a tall chrysanthemum wood.
The flowers dipped their heads and began to scream,
I fled and reached a chocolate stream.
As I crossed it something snapped at my heel,
I was about to become giant tadpole meal.
So I ran and ran with all my might,
Until I came to an awful sight.
A butterfly eating a crocodile,
I squealed and a cow jumped over a stile.
I awoke with a start from my nightmarish dream,
And laughed as I realised what had been.

*P Kendrick*


## Looking Back

As we began,
How we did plan,
        So young and eager.

Time passes,
We need glasses,
        Older and wiser

Memories to hold,
With threads of gold,
        To recall.

As we sit and reflect,
On every aspect,
    often a smile.

It wasn't too bad,
So we can be glad,
    Time lent and how well spent?

**Myrtle Holmes**


## A MEAL FIT FOR . . . HUMAN CONSUMPTION?

My husband cooked the tea last night
He said I needed rest
He made a stew, and yes I knew
He really did his best.

He sat me down and served it up
He really had done well,
Not only did it look like food,
It had a foodie smell.

As keen as sin, I tucked right in
Expecting it was tasty,
But all too soon I realised
That I had been too hasty.

I smiled at him and sweetly asked
What was his key ingredient?
He said 'Just eat it up my dear'
I had to be obedient.

When later on I searched the bin
I found he'd used the mustard,
But worse than that - I almost spat,
He'd thickened it with custard!

***Kerry-Ann Howitt***

# SHE DID NO WRONG

I close my eyes what do I see
This poor little girl upon my knee
Big blue eyes shoulder length hair
She sheepishly whispered 'My name is Clare.'

Her once shattered face was healing quite well
But still full of pain it was easy to tell
A clumsy hook where her hand should be
She'd lost her right leg below the knee.

This poor little girl had done nothing at all
She was out with her brother playing ball
Causing no trouble committing no crime
She was in the wrong place it being the wrong time.

All the killing and destruction too
But it's never to late to start anew
For this poor little girl she got in the way
Of a mindless gang called the IRA.

### David Webster


# MILLENNIUM CARGO

Fabricated cargo from the north of Russia
Growling through a blizzard on an ink-black night.
Onward to rail heads
Of western approaches
Buried for an aeon on a toxic site.

Ocean liner sparkling in the silky sunlight
Snorting in the morning at the tug boat crews
Gangways swarming
With ant-like travellers
Docking to normality and homespun news.

Predatory tanker on the rip tide lurching
Slapping the containers in the oil-filled hull
Draining every terminal
Piped from the sea bed
Sinister and waiting for the bright-eyed gull.

*Clive Macdonald*


## GROWING OLD

Life grows dim as one grows old
Your legs get stiff you feel the cold
The days and weeks just seem to fly
Time so quickly passes by

You sit and think about the past
The days of youth that went so fast
Of errands run for neighbour or friend
Of a penny reward for you to spend

School days your cap short trousers too
Jobs for mum we had to do
The walk to school no cars then
Home for dinner then back again

Memories some good some bad
Your time at work the fun we had
The girls we dated through the years
Joy and laughter toil and tears

Happy thoughts of things we did
Of pals we knew when we were kids
On the whole it's not so bad
Growing old is just sad

*G Emery*

## CHILDHOOD DREAMS

Take my hand, guide me through my childhood dreams
From tin toy planes
To hide and seek games
And long summer days of hope.

Don't feel sorry for me
If you hear whispers through doors
Telling of my parentless past
And my lone lost wars.

Guide me through my humbug days
And wicked ways.
Mrs Henmon's sherbet lemons
Geoffrey Chaucer's flying saucers.

Lord, guide me through my childhood dreams
Through large oak doors
Down dark corridors
Leaving this world behind me.

*Rod Stalham*


## PRECIOUS MOMENTS

The sun revolves around us
And time moves on so fast,
Grasp your precious moments
For nothing here will last.

Least of all our presence,
As we live beneath the sun,
Time is long but life is short
From whence we first began.

So hold each moment tenderly,
Through laughter and through pain,
The precious moment passing by,
Will not return again.

*Carole Wood*


## A LOST FRIEND

You lovely fluffy pussycat
what can I do to get you back?
I miss the way you talk to me
you purr and purr so perfectly.
You wash your paws and clean your ears;
the loss of you brings many tears.
I've asked the neighbours to check their sheds
in case you entered when they turned their heads.
I've searched the village, hedgerows and verge
calling your name, hoping you'd emerge.
I've published posters and displayed them around.
Please come back to patrol your home ground.
No one has seen you, where can you be?
I'm here in the house waiting for tea.
I've cooked you chicken, your favourite meal.
Please come in and brush against my heel.
I want to hold you, stroke your fur.
I want to cuddle you whilst you purr.
I want you to wink your eyes at me.
I want you here where I can see.
It's three days now that you've been missing
I've said many prayers and keep on wishing.
Are you being naughty chasing the rabbits?
Or practising lazy sleeping habits?
Whatever you're doing I want you back home
I can't bear the thought of living alone.

*Carole Backham*

## DANIELLE

When Danielle was born, she didn't have a dad,
The birth you see was rather sad,
Her father didn't want to know
And watch his baby daughter grow.

His flight took him across the sea,
But in his mind it will always be,
Her birth was long and painful too,
But Danielle was wanted so her mum saw it through.

When she was born and laid close to breast
The tears did flow with new 'mum's' happiness.
Baby cried so much, and seemed to know,
Dad wasn't there for mum to show.

But many friends came round to call,
With cards and flowers and presents from all,
So much to do, a new mouth to feed,
Care lavished upon her every need.

Nanna and granddad gave their support,
Baby equipment they went and bought.
Their first grandchild was loved so well,
Pictures were taken and friends to tell.

Danielle's so beautiful with eyes deep blue,
A good head of hair, looks like mummy too,
What life will bring it's for us to see,
We will cushion the blows with our love you and me.

*Clare Bright*

## BEYOND SENSE OF ROAD

Rocking car clambers
Gravelly pass.
We peer out thrilling
At precarious drops.
Rain scratches the glass.

Charcoal-smudged sky
Like an artist's page.
Mountains are women,
Softness and bone
Bleached with age.

Perpetual wedding veils,
Crushed velvet dresses.
A skeleton's hand
Stretched miles to shore's rock,
Smooth with caresses.

Dark hollows of skull,
Sea's skirt laps the land,
Breakers like petticoats.
Mirror spoilt with unsilvering
The reflecting wet sand.

Of jasper blue, lemon.
We are balanced in air.
Clouds measure out time,
We sense the eternal
For a moment there.

*Catherine Rose*

## REVISING DRAFTS

She was in at the beginning.
My first draft emerged
like a snail from its shell under her bright bird eyes.
I wrote for her sitting touched by her shadow
in the patch of warmth we had left in our duvet.

She deleted
pecking the paper with red ink.
She taught - *some things are scaffolding.*
*They are only aids to get you started.*
She enjoyed picking threads, unravelling cloth,
pursuing a frayed strand across a bright surface.

I followed her fingers, I watched them editing
my underpants, my socks,
my friends from my diary,
slowly but surely she took me apart
winding me up into neat balls of twine.

My second draft came slowly emerging like a bruise
I had been forced into recognising mistakes.
I parroted.

*Does that have to be kept?*

I wrote on and realised that I was not writing a romance.

She was in at the beginning
but she hasn't stayed to the end.
I will enjoy deleting her completely from my final draft.

*Gavin Stewart*

# I'M STILL HERE
*(In loving memory of Donald Maurice Goodchild)*

Even though you think I've gone,
You couldn't be so much more wrong,
I'm still here,
I can handle your fears.
Just remember me,
Through your memories.
When you walk out of your door
I am the rush of winds that follow,
I will follow you where ever you go,
As you are safe and never alone.
Maybe you can't see me,
But you can all feel me,
As I'm like the flower in your garden,
But instead I grow in your heart.
Now I've left this earth,
To go to a better place,
We will all meet up again,
I'm waiting for that day.

***Victoria Hunt  (13)***


# YOU FROM ME

Like bluebells you shine right into my eyes,
That special look that's so divine,
A smile so big it makes my heart sink beneath,
I hold you so tight I can hardly breathe,
Deep breaths I take to put myself at ease,
I'm sure you'll return, this isn't the end,
Please come back, on you I depend.

***Nicola Walker***

## COASTAL ZONE BABY

Baby bird-song lullaby dreamer
Gypsy dancing at the Mad Hatter's Waltz
Breeze-waving, free-forming in furtive foam
Wallowing in the mellowing shallows
Honey-curls, yogic feline of silken textures
Soft-skinned coastal zone baby
Lushing with lust-flipping tingles
Happy elfin child, showering in sparkling star dust
Snowflake shaper, basking in the mother sun
Racing whispers across unfathomable pastures

Slanting a pathway into the blinking horizon
Floating through a tapestry of delight
Skipping along golden rails
In a bohemian train, full of alien concepts
On a galactic holiday of exotic investigation
Spiralling through layers of submerged eroticism
Catching droplets of ecstasy in the moonlit joy
Intoxicated with the ether of adventure
Gazing into the distance, still swimming with energy
In the vibrating pools of mysterious pleasure.

*Matthew W Jones*


## THE STORM

I saw a rainbow in the sky,
Birds flying way up high,
Gentle sounds in the breeze,
Butterflies and humming bees.

Then the wind and rain does come,
I say goodbye to the sun,
The lightning flashes, I do shudder,
Then there is a crash of thunder.

The rain is coming down so fast,
But very soon it will pass,
The sun will come out quite soon,
Revealing a lovely afternoon.

*L Osborne*

## YELLOW HAT DAY

When I was young and carefree
And mornings not completely frost-free,
As the breeze was blowing, swiftly, while
The blossom billowed blithely;
How the spring days so entranced me!
and I trimmed a yellow hat,
With silken flowers, wildly,
And I stitched a cotton skirt
To twirl all around me.

When the days were brightly sailing
And the hawthorn scent bewitching,
When the birds were busy nesting
And wilful clouds a-trailing
Then I wore my yellow hat
So absolutely sweetly
On my softly yellow hair.

Now, when the May days sparkle, brightly
And the bees are surely seeking
I hear my mother's voice,
Quite distinctly, speaking
Calling to me gently,
Down and down the years:
'The sun is shining gaily,
So wear your yellow hat.'

**D Wain**

## PEGGY SMALLRIDGE'S BENCH

Many times I walk and like to sit where you are rested.
I don't know why I want to talk to you,
In search of an answer perhaps.

I search to feel your presence
And while I am still,
Nothing I feel; not the midday sun warming my face
Nothing I hear, not the leaves rustled by the gentle breeze
Nothing I see, not the many colours of the sky,
Nothing, just me sitting and thinking.

Are you the bench of life
Or just trees chopped down
To have tired bodies rest
In the walk of the reserve.

And still I search for your presence.
Are you . . . I think it's me,
Looking for a feeling, an unknown feeling
In the darkness in the light.

Maybe I am looking the wrong way.
I find joy looking into my children's eyes.
I find joy looking at my lovely wife.
Something has touched my mind . . .

. . . It's probably me.

I like to thank you
To let me rest and talk
To let me search and find nothing
I like to thank you for being there
To let me rest and think.

*Ludovico Scaletta*

## JUMP

I'm going to jump, honest.
I promised myself that I would.
I knew that I could,
Though they think that I won't.
But I'm going to jump, you see if I don't.

I'm going to jump, with pride,
And glide through the air I'm leaving.
I've got my reasons,
Personal atonement.
I'm going to jump, away in a moment.

There's quite a crowd now, down there.
Around where I'm heading, below me.
They do not know me,
And most will soon forget,
But I'm going to jump, jump off in a sec.

And I don't like heights you know,
I get vertigo on ladders me.
Who's here as mad as me?
This ledge is far too small.
But I'm going to jump or else I shall fall.

I jumped, and dropped and screamed and stopped.
And rose and then I fell again.
Oh how they swooned and my senses swam,
As ground snapped back to the bungee twang.

And as I dangled on the elastic,
I thought about life
Waiting for the man to wind me down.
And as I vomited back my breakfast,
I though now that I've jumped, I could be that chap,
In control of the line.

*Ian Dixon*

## HIGHLAND HOSPITALITY

One morning in late October, when the weather was none too good
We went for a drive through areas where many brave men once
stood,
We saw waterfalls in distant hills and craggy mountain tops,
Burnished browns and autumn gold were on the mountains for all
to see and behold,
The trees with their golden crowns, the ferns, brackens and grass took
on the autumnal hues,
And as the mist swirled round the mountain tops
A buzzard hovered, his thoughts on prospective prey.
Haunting, atmospheric music evoked thoughts of a long ago day
Of these brave men marching o'er the hills.
And as we stopped at Glenfinnan where the Young Pretender raised
his standard,
The weather brightened though the clouds still gathered,
As we stood and soaked in the atmosphere and viewed the wondrous
scene
And I felt humbled to think that I was here where once Charles Edward
Stuart had been.

As we continued on our way it became quite bleak,
But, as so often happens, a while later the clouds lifted once more
And the scenic vistas came again into view
With waters cascading in full spate down the mountainsides
Then behind the clouds the brightness again hides,
As we travel on through wild, remote beauty
To have lunch at a hotel owned by a local man,
Full of character he was, shaking hands with everyone as in we went,
His greeting and welcome evidently well meant.

It was an experience I personally was very pleased to have had,
To enjoy the Highlands hospitality I was very glad,
But we had to travel on and eventually return on the same road we came
Back to our 'home', to view the distant islands once more,
To hold in my memory the magical scenes of the day
And hope in my heart that once again I'll come this way.

*Lesley Stevenson*

## CHRISTMAS WISH

I've had my bath with nanny's help, she's awfully good at those,
She does the hard bits like my hair, and dries between my toes.
I've had my supper biscuit, and a lovely milky drink,
Nan says it's time to settle down and have a little think!
Cos soon it will be Christmas, and we'll need to know for sure
If there's something special we must ask old Santa for.
The window in my bedroom looks over Peter's wall,
Sometimes, at the weekends, we watch them playing ball
When Peter's daddy kicks it, it goes almost to the sky,
You wouldn't think a football could ever go so high!
My mummy can't play football, she just can't kick it straight,
'Sides, it muddies up her stockings, and her shoes get in a state.
But she's very good at cuddles, and kissing bumps away.
We always end up laughing, whatever games we play.
I've had so many uncles I've forgotten all their names,
Still, they're never really friendly, or know the proper games.
So, if Santa Claus is listening, and would like to make me glad,
The bestest thing that he could do is . . . magic me a dad.

*Anthony D Parker*

## A PRICE TO PAY

Abuse to a child is the ultimate sin,
You take from the world, a wonderful thing,
How can things go forward, when we cease to see.
The next generation were once you and me.

As children, though older,
We can learn from our own.
The mistakes that we made
When we felt all alone.

In the struggle to do right
In a world that seemed wrong.
For our children, God bless them
To know right from wrong.

To credit the children
When shown the true way,
To use their new knowledge
And please! Have their say.

Not wait 'til they're grown up,
Like you and me,
Before they're allowed,
To voice all that they see.

They have pure clear vision
Which we may have lost
In trying too hard
To achieve for them *most!*

*June Chorlton*

# THE ROAD FORWARD

Children of tomorrow, listen to me today
I want to tell you something that may help you on your way
Soon you will travel on the road I've already walked
Perhaps you'll meet some wise men to whom I have often talked
You'll be faced with mountains, you will have to climb
I'll pray that your problems won't be as big as mine
Don't think you're too small to listen as soon as you learn to read
Listen to your teachers, their advice will always lead
To better ways, to happy days when you will achieve
The first steps, the very first steps, to what you'll believe
Will be your future world, your world so safe with dad and mum
But with no dad and mum (not so good for some)
Still for most of you, it will be up to you
Whatever your dreams, whatever your schemes
The answer is work, to study and work
No excuses, no lies, it's weakness to shirk,
So right from the start, you be one of the wise
No matter your looks, your colour or size
Make up your mind, you'll not be a worm, or mix with slugs
Don't waste your time on daydreamers or drugs
From time to time things may look black
You'll feel your efforts wasted and tempted to slack
Lift up your head, be proud of your way
Then bow your head, be humble and pray
Pray for guidance, pray for strength
I've been on that road, (in despair) the whole length
But I did not give in, still worked (while I cried)
One day my prayers were answered, and I looked back with pride
So children, climb your tallest tree, cling on to that limb
In English 'without God you have nothing,' in Welsh, that reads
                    'Heb Dduw - Heb DDim.'

*Millicent Colwell*

## NEAR LITTON CHENEY

I look back and what do I see?
Much that charms and does feelingly agree;
A tableau of the old millennium
Calmly waiting for the next to come continuum.

Green hills there are speckled with sheep,
Grazing lazily on the fields laid steep;
But where the land allows the tractor to go,
Patches of white etched by the plough.

Lower down before the valley's water catch,
A Doomsday village nestles stone and thatch;
With the church beaconing its ray,
Harbouring all in its influence and say.

Along the top, flat as a rustic table,
Traffic glides modern live to enable;
Silent, exhaustless, as tropical fish relaxing serene,
Capping the scene defining the green.

All is quiet in the village too,
Frenzied activity to eschew;
But near by children play joyfully at school,
In tension theirs is the coming world to tool.

How future dawns will arise from the mist
Is beyond anyone's sure prediction and forecasting gift;
But from afar change will certainly occur,
Presaged there with the sight of the car.

May the valley preserve that which is good,
And progress its destiny thoughtfully understood;
From local stone and homely thatch,
May not our senses widely dispatch.

*E Ashwell*

## REFLECTIONS

Reflections floating in the pool
Of the sky, the clouds, the trees,
Then the mirror image shimmers
Broken by a playful breeze.
The swallows skimming gracefully,
A swift, dark shadow shows.
Then all is calm and smooth again
The pool's in deep repose.
Life itself is like a pool
Events are reflected there.
Happiness is light and sweet
And all the world is fair.
But troubles come disturbing
And cast reflections deep,
Dark shadows showing in the glass
Like nightmares during sleep.
One's image in the looking glass
Reflects the years gone by
The laugher lines, the slightest frown,
It never tells a lie.
Reflecting back upon one's life,
Don't dwell upon the troubles
But pick out all the happy times
You'll find their memory doubles.
Let your mind be like the pool
Don't look for trouble and strife,
Then like the peaceful water,
It will reflect the best in life.

*Ruth Purdy*

## HISTORY PORTRAYED

The painting of a picture speaks
        more than words can say,
Reflected in the artist's strokes, are
        feelings sad and gay.
Memories implanted, by love, tenderness
        and care,
Are preserved for future records, of
        things historical and rare.
The pictures tell a story, depending
        on your point of view,
But what it tells to others, may not
        be the same for you.
With earnest contemplation of the
        paintings you behold,
One thinks about the cavemen, when
        they, their way of life foretold.
They had no books or manuscripts,
        or a pencil or a pen,
To record the happenings, of their
        progress there and then.
And yet we know their history recorded
        for us all,
They used their knives and pointed tools
        to scribe pictures on cave walls.
These pictures told a story for the
        future of mankind,
Which now we can see and understand,
        from these drawings that we find.

*L Barnes*

# A PLEASURE GONE

There was a lovely skating rink,
Up on the London road,
Where all we youngsters used to meet,
With a strict no-nonsense code.

It started up before the war,
We girls and boys would go,
To see how long we stayed upright,
As our skills we tried to show.

After a while we got quite good,
At skating round and round,
And over lemonade, we knew,
A fine sport we had found.

Turning and twisting was a thrill,
Our confidence was high,
But what we skaters didn't know,
Its time was flying by.

Into our lives there came the war,
The rink just had to be shut,
To make the parts the planes would need,
to shut old Hitler up.

Lots of us who met there, were wed
During that awful time,
And had to separate for years,
It was a dreadful crime.

Last week my man and I went back,
To see that rink once more,
But it had gone, demolished flat,
It really made us sore.

*Isobel Crumley*

## An Old Soldier's Thoughts

Don't talk to me of glory, when the drums begin to roll,
Just remind me of the shot and shell that takes its deadly toll
When, standing four square 'gainst the lance,
Each man a frightened pawn of chance,
Who didn't want to be there,
Who didn't want to die.

Don't talk to me of glory, when the bugle starts to play,
Just count the cost in mothers' sons at the ending of the day,
When, ten thousand men went o'er the top
Through wire and mud they wouldn't stop.
They didn't want to be there,
They didn't want to die.

Don't talk to me of glory when the pipes begin to skirl,
Just see the kilted soldier who will never wed his girl.
Through sea and sand he led the way.
The beach-head made that longest day.
But he didn't want to be there,
He didn't want to die.

Yes, talk to me of glory, when the Battle Honours fly,
For each one tells a story, of men who didn't want to die.
For some went home and others stayed
In God's green earth their bodies laid.
They didn't want to be there,
They didn't want to die.

So when the Last Post echoes, on some November morn,
Remember those across the years who did not live to mourn,
Read faceless names engraved in stone,
Of those who never made it home,
Though they had to be there,
Did they have to die?

*G Simmonds*

## SHE'S THE GUN

She's the gun
You're the bullet
Her trigger's sensitive
Take care not to pull it
Or with a bang she'll shoot you through
At a hundred miles per hour
She'll say goodbye to you.

She's the gun
She will remain
Though in her chamber and empty space
It won't be long
Before the bullet's replaced.

And as for you
A burnt out fuse
An empty shell
Crumpled and used.

*J O'Donnell*


## BE(E)HAVIOUR

Spare a thought for the busy bee
making honey for our breakfast and tea
just think how the creature spends all those hours
buzzing between oh so many flowers

Later on though it's back to the hive
where the young ones and the queen do thrive
*she* keeps her hair looking shiny
is it the (honey)comb she uses? Maybe!

**James V Hooton**

## THE CHURCH CAT

He prowls the graveyard in the night,
Then vanishes before it's light
To sit with piety divine,
Awaiting (some say) a sacred sign,
From 'him above'.

He eyes the tiny harvest mouse,
Who scuttles to his cosy house
Among the ancient oozing hassocks,
Hoping to chew discarded cassocks,
Long left behind.

But after evensong is done,
And when the congregation's gone,
Then, he gives a throaty growl,
And sets out for his nightly prowl,
Among the dead.

*Elizabeth Branston*


## MY LOVE

Come walk this
Gentle masquerade
With me
Put your mask on
To mystify your true love.
Come, rejoice in truth
And not truth
Today and not today.
Play each part well
with me.
For we can bear
Each other's birth.

*Mary Elizabeth Percy-Burns*

# BEAUTY AND THE BEAST
*(There is a beast that dwells within us all)*

She was a thing of beauty peering through the undergrowth
As the sun caught and glinted on her rich, red coat.
Her ears were pricked taking in the far off sounds,
It might mean *danger!* But to her 'twas still remote.

The woman too, had hair of russet red
And looked a picture in her coat of 'hunting pink'
The milling hounds were ready to be away
it was time for the hunt to have that final drink.

The vixen was the reason for this hunt today,
Though really of an excuse there was never any need,
But she was the thief that had killed the farmer's hen
Rabbits were scarce; she had hungry cubs to feed.

She was out hunting again for her growing young
When in the distance she heard the baying hound,
It had her scent, and cunning as she might be,
She was tiring, and there was little cover to be found.

At last the coppice with a gully and a stream
Where she crossed the scent of a dog fox on her way
To safety, while the pack followed the other scent.
She'd been reprieved - at least for another day.

The hunt was successful. The pack had made a kill.
After 'blooding' a lad the Master let the hounds 'feast'.
And the woman laughed when she received 'the brush'.
Beauty was dead, all that remained was 'The Beast'.

*Hannah M French*

# NORTH DEVON

North Devon I long to be,
Westward Ho and the clear blue sea,
Huge boulders on the beach,
The waves splashing but can't quite reach,
The one thing I remember most,
The sandy beaches of this beautiful coast.
Ilfracombe is where I love to stay,
It's quiet but friendly, I like it that way.
A little place called Appledore
I've been there a few times before,
But the one place I love to go,
Clovelly, ooh I adore it so.
It's very cobbled and very old,
The fishermen love it so I'm told,
It's a place that is very steep,
The people who live there regularly sweep.
There are tiny cottages, that flowers colour,
A place of beauty there is no other.
There are donkeys with carts to help those in need,
A picturesque place, oh yes indeed.

*Sally Swain*


## WALSALL MARKET

He moves through the market, selling his wares.
With a tingle of music as he moves here and there.
All men are equal, all men have rights.
The tea-pot man, he has inner sight.
In his land they are waiting
waiting to see, who he will be bringing,
bringing for tea.

*Roy Storey*

## PATTERNS OF TENDER THOUGHT

We who have loved approach to greet
Each other with our fond support.
Some who have lost feel more complete.

Those frantic lives with business fraught,
Are steadied by those whose hearts now beat
In slower rhythm, by patience taught.

Waves of affection around us meet,
Flowing and smoothing till they're as naught
The clumsy, the brash, the indiscreet.

Our greatest treasure, once keenly sought,
Was even the patter of tiny feet;
Now mellower company's rendered sweet,
By patterns of tender thought.

*Sylvia Tyers*


## ROSES

Your petal's so soft, just like velvet
delicate to touch
Sweet aromas from your fragrance
And loved very much
A variety of beautiful colours
Each one bearing a name
Grown and sent world-wide
Celebrating different occasions.

Roses capture more hearts
Than any other flower
Bringing love, happiness and
romance into someone's life.

*Sharyn Waters*

# THE FARM ON THE HILL

With a pipe in his mouth,
His old dog at his knee,
They sit in the shade
Of the old apple tree.
And watching, I know,
They are both of them still,
In thoughts, roaming free,
At the farm on the hill.

When the rosy dawn broke
They have counted their flock,
With the dew on their feet
While the valley lay still,
And when evening came
The bright moon looking down
Lit their weary path home
To the farm on the hill.

Sharing good times and bad,
They have plodded their way
Through snow inches deep
While the wind whistles shrill,
And many a lamb who had wandered astray
Owed his life to their care,
At the farm on the hill.

With his pipe in his mouth,
The old dog at his knee,
Till the end of their lives,
Together they'll be,
And when the time comes
Their spirits will still
Be guardians two, at the
Farm on the hill.

*Joyce Mussett*

# EARLY SATURDAY MORNING TRAIN TO KINGS CROSS

The early train just after dawn,
Some passengers discreetly yawn.
Ely's cathedral seen to loom,
Emerging through the misty gloom.
The train onward goes, wheels turning,
On to Cambridge, seat of learning.
Then quiet stations, newly swept,
Somnolence over all has crept.
Calmly, no immediate rush,
Not fully awake, dreamlike hush.
Different view now taking shape,
Gaudy patches of golden rape,
Like bits of sunshine left behind.
Lush green meadows and lanes that wind.
Several new towns whose newness
Looks a little worn, lustreless.
Train glides onwards, out of the sticks,
Town outskirts, grime encrusted bricks.
Sounding above the engine's groans,
Through the speaker, a voice intones
'Arrival at Kings Cross now due,
Change, take everything with you.'
Spilling from automated doors,
Noise to the station rooftop soars
A surge and the clatter of feet,
London's awake, into the street,
Where the bustle brings nostalgia,
And a special kind of aura.

*Lilian Owen*

## NOW THAT YOU'RE GONE

I see the world in black and white
now that you're gone.
I'm faced with stark reality
now that you're gone.
There are no sunny days.
No morning light.
There's only black and white,
now that you're gone.
No songbirds soar in my dark sky,
No flowers bloom,
No breezes sigh.
No fluffy clouds to float on high.
No rainbow arch nor silver Moon.
Around me time and tide moves on,
But life itself for me has gone,
My world, in black and white, stands still,
I see no other colours now,
Now that you're gone.

*Jenny Porteous*


## THE LAST ROSE

When summer fades, and days grow short,
And fruits are gathered in and stored.
Yet on a rosebush grows a bud,
A golden gift, a treasured hoard.

A bloom so perfect in its form.
A child of summer sun and shower.
Enclosing petals, velvet wrapped
In curving folds, a jewel flower.

Now as the season's cold approach,
Makes pruning of this bush a need.
Yet still in cupped perfection there,
Half opened, scented, beauty's creed.

*Margery Selby*


## THE SWALLOWS

The old barn roof their gathering place,
Small groups swelled until a seethe
Of sheeny fervent joyous life
With tiny hearts attuned to leave.
The waves of raucous comrades went,
Drowning me in silence.
The swallows left today.

Swallows love and live long summer through,
Know just when to pick their joy
And also know when summer's gone.
When evening's breath is damply cool,
Before the chill can slow their hearts,
They know it's time to go.
The swallows left today.

I've watched the swallows' summer joy
Soar on breeze, cavort in sun,
But kept my dreams in shaded place,
Shut out day before day's done,
Yet craved summer that did not come.
Now one more summer's gone.
The swallows left today.

*Sylvia Anne Lees*

## SIMPLY, REALLY, ALWAYS

Simply not feeling right,
simply not me.
Simply staying awake at night,
simply trying to be.

Really only sane,
really is all I can take.
Really no one to blame,
really I need a break.

Always need direction,
always from above.
Always want some perfection,
always we need love.

*Anne V Westwood*


## WORLD AT HIS FEET

Sadness in his eye
To a meeting of the senses
On the cosmic plain
To a crossing of the way
His head and mind
In focus with his image.
A world at his feet
Of rational stability
Among the green and gold
Of his harvest
Of reaped reward.

*Roger Thornton*

## BELONGING TO SOMEBODY ELSE

The window's open, the lights are bright
and I can still see her from the bedroom window.
My window that waits for a different view,
each and every same day.
The TV's stopped, no power over me anymore.
It buzzes with its white light and speckled haze.
Images waiting to appear onto my already muddled brain.
And yet I still see her as she is from my bedroom window.
Lost clothes from another tomorrow, that past yesterday.
A dress, too long.
I light a cigarette, wet on my lips
longing for her feelings to know mine too,
as I watch her from my bedroom window,
no longer there.
I have that dress. I wear it sometimes, with the
memories it held in our skin.
It ages with me, keeping up at a pace I fear will overtake,
and find a new lover, younger than me.
I would not blame her, for she's waiting too
for the TV to flicker and show her new sights.
New power.
New light, brighter than me.
But as I wait now, cigarette still burning, at the window
I see a different view.
Not her, but the TV, power restored.
Not her, power restored
Not her, not at my window, not in our dress
belonging to somebody else.

*C R Reynolds*

## EVENING FIELD

The air's full of bird song and munching of cows,
      'Neath the hedge there are bluebells and cow-parsley too,
It's the end of the day, the sun is still warm
      And the blue sky is ringed with the sunset's red hue.

I stand in this field where my fathers once stood
      And my heart's beating firmly as theirs once did too.
Then I think of the years of heartache and toil
      That have gone into making this Staffordshire view.

A curlew is calling above the clear stream.
      There's a flash as a mouse scuttles over the lane.
As I watch, a red fox just slips through my hedge,
      Then he lopes down my field on his track once again.

My hedges I tend as my fathers once did,
      There, the birds and the animals always may hide.
There the wild rose and the honeysuckle bloom
      And the pink spotted foxgloves stand tall there with pride.

I've been up since sunrise pushed back the night sky,
      I have milked and I've silaged, examined the grain,
I've repaired tractor engines, cleaned up the yard;
      I've been pleased with the sunshine, but hope for some rain.

But this is *my* field and in wonder I stand,
      As my father and his both in wonder stood too.
As my body aches gently from the day's work,
      Sweet peace courses my veins when I look at this view.

Yes, this is my field, in my trust and my care.
      My forefathers were here since before time began,
Their blood sings in my veins. Just look at this field!
      It's a Staffordshire field! I'm a proud farming man!

*Sheila E Harvey*

## MACKENZIE ROAD

Why did two art dealers select
This cheerless road in which to work?
Patches of ugly wasteland stare.
Houses, suggesting bygone pride,
Stand unattractive: modern ones
Reveal no sense of artistry.
Its dwellers are mundane, sometimes
Unkempt, and cosmopolitan.

But many years ago these men,
Inspired, resolved to brighten it,
And in their warehouse window placed
Three paintings, valuable, fine,
And several costly ornaments.

Over the years, from week to week,
The pictures have been changed. New works
And older: portraits, flowers, scenes
In oils; landscapes in water-colours
Have appeared. Bronze statuettes,
Elegant bowls and ornaments
From foreign parts, have been displayed.

Most people pass without a pause,
But others, who must walk that way,
Do so in expectation of
The latest treasures for their minds.
They leave that tiny gallery,
And tread the dull, unsmiling street
With lighter steps, and feel towards
Those public-minded art dealers
A glow of warmth and gratitude.

*Dora Hawkins*

## WETLEY ROCKS' WI MILLENNIUM BUG

### Complacency

'Time waits for no one' our President said,
'So thinking caps pulled please onto your heads.'
Last November we began to think perhaps just a little,
But thirteen months on - well ladies are fickle!

### Thinking

'Any ideas yet?' we were asked in the middle of December,
But Christmas was near we'd got presents to remember.
A year away now, so there's plenty of time,
It wasn't as if we'd got mountains to climb.

### Worrying

January's here now and we'd better get cracking,
Eleven months to go so there'd better be no slacking.
A meeting was held by our small happy few,
We talked and we talked and we drank tea - phew.

### Beginning

Ten months away, and our WI is still fretting,
To see what contribution the village will be getting.
A wall hanging is agreed upon as a colourful feature,
I wish I'd taken more notice of my school sewing teacher!

### Working

March, marches on and we're still beavering away,
A few are quite happy, but some have gone grey!
Here is the church, school, chapel and hall,
Gosh! How do you stitch a lovely stone wall?

### Progressing

Nine months away, no it's not a baby we're hatching,
This embroidery lark can get really quite catching.
Each person has created something quite new,
When it's finished we hope it will be liked by you.

Finished

I cannot predict what it will look like when it's sewn,
When we've got tired eyes and fingers worked to the bone.
We've all tried our best to contribute in some way,
Let's hope it is ready for the Millennium Day.

Love

But most of all sewn in that fabric is Hope,
Hope for the future, for family and friends,
Peace for our children as this Millennium ends,
Peace for the world as a new one begins.

*Pauline A Kelsall*


## JEKYLL AND HYDE

Your sleek and shining black fur coat,
Your twitching ears, alert and ever sharp.
Your eyes so bright, observe and take a note -
Of the pond, with gleaming golden carp.
Your body crouched, ready to leap at will,
The tail erect or flicking side to side.
The creeping form, edging with such skill -
You pounce, but the little bird can fly.
Then you appear to have no interest in your prey,
And with your head aloof, pause, and walk away.
But there's another side of you I see -
A purring friendly little cat.
When you look up with big green eyes at me -
You are my pet, and I am very glad of that.

*J Carr*

# COVENTRY PAST

With three spires standing tall
Medieval shops and St Mary's hall
Peeping Tom and of course
Lady Godiva on her horse
This Coventry is of a bygone age
Let us now look at the present stage
        Coventry present
After the end of World War Two
Coventry was rebuilt anew
New shops appeared upon the scene
Museums were visited by the Queen
The people of Coventry take great pride
In the old and new cathedrals standing side by side.
        Coventry Future
As we approach the year 2,000
What does the future hold in store?
Do we celebrate with fireworks
Or should we wait to learn the score
It will give us all a dreadful fright
If the millennium bug decides to bite
But whatever happens I'm sure we'll cope
For Coventry people never give up hope.

*Joan Jones*

# THE RED ADMIRAL

Hairy little creature
I often wonder why,
I see you in a jam-jar
Perhaps left there to die.

I will gently lift you
to a leafy tree so high.
Then maybe in a day or two
you will be a lovely *Butterfly!*

**Beryl Holroyd-Fidler**


## ALAN REMEMBERED

Ram-a-lam-a ding-dong, shooby doo wop
There ain't no cure for the summertime blues.
Sounds and words remembered with love
But who remembers you?

You helped the kids do their thing
Authority slammed you for it
And just when it seemed you were winning through
You were dumped and made to pay the forfeit.

This devil's music really isn't as bad
As some people tried to make out
It's merely a way of letting off steam
For those with expressions to shout.

With courage and vision you did what you thought
When others thought you were wrong
You risked prosecution and the loss of your job
To bring us a new musical tongue.

Mr Rock 'n' Roll, our thanks to you
The change you effected was in need
Your child of the fifties has grown, how it's grown
To honour its father, Alan Freed.

**Peter Fletcher**

# A PAINTER WRITES A LOVE LETTER

I have painted a chair for you to sit on
I have painted a table for you to eat at
I have painted for you a book
to read by lamp-light after the day's work.

I have painted a window for you
to look out of in the morning
with a sky to look up to
and white clouds travelling across it
which I have painted for you
to follow with your eyes
and with your dreams.

I have painted a gate for you
into a garden that I have also painted
for you to stroll in
and I have painted in it a tree
for you to breathe deeply in its shade;
it is age-old and gnarled
and it has turned out to be an apple tree.
So I have painted this apple on it,
for you to pick and savour.

In a corner of the garden is a bush.
It is a rose bush.
I have just finished it.

And I am now painting a dark red rose onto it
with a white spot to indicate sunlight.
In a slender silver vase that I intend to paint for you
presently,
you may put it in front of you on the table
with the lamp and the book.

But where shall I find a pigment
to convey to you its perfume?

*Kate Fielding*

# A PICTURE

We have a beautiful picture
Of Jesus hanging on our wall
As He sits amongst His sheep
His smile beams upon us all.

He listens to us laughing
And when we need to cry
But I know He is with us
From His heaven in the sky.

God gave to us His son
To learn us how to pray
Who gave to us great love
And shown us the true way.

When He was upon the cross
The pain He did endure
To cleanse us of our sins
And make us all so pure.

But some of us have strayed
From His father up above
Let's get back upon His path
Then He'll shower us with love.

Yes we have a lovely picture
Of Jesus hanging on our wall
As He sits amongst His sheep
His smile beams upon us all.

*David Brownley*

## MY HOLIDAY

The dramatic hills of Ireland
And its lovely Kilarney Lake,
With its breathtaking scenery
To keep you wide awake,
Driving up the mountain side
To the top of Healey Pass,
The stunning view from on high
Nothing can surpass,
That lovely Emerald Isle
Across the Irish Sea,
The welcome of the friendly folk
Make it great for me,
We visited Iralee
And dear old Galway Bay,
Queen's View and Dingle Peninsula's
With its rocks so grey,
God sure did make old Ireland
And its true what they say,
When you visit the Emerald Isle
You will return one day.

*Alice Stapleton*


## REMEMBER THOSE IN NEED

It is easy to forget,
Cocooned in our island home,
Those who are left entirely alone.

It is easy to forget,
With our well-stocked fridge and freezer,
Those who suffer the agonies of hunger.

It is easy to forget,
As we turn on the taps so carelessly,
Those who need water so desperately.

It is easy to forget,
When concerned with trivialities,
Those living in fear of brutalities.

So let us not forget,
But do our best to remember,
And help where we can for relief far asunder.

*Mary Marriott*

## A SPECIAL COUPLE

There are two people on this Earth, one of them was at my birth;
The other came later in life, and took the first one for his wife:

They mean so very much to me, and helped me be who I ought to be;
Sometimes I stray and I am bad, and I know this makes them
sometimes sad:

I love them both as they do each other, my stepfather and my mother;
I'm grateful for everything they do . . . and have done;
They're also my friends and are so much fun:

I'm proud of them and tell all my mates;
They've always helped me when I've made mistakes:

I know that I am a moody and a mardy child;
And maybe sometimes a little wild;
But I don't mean to be selfish and unkind;
And they've found my feelings sometimes hard to find:

I don't always hug them or give them a kiss;
But I do still love them and it's them I'd miss:
If ever they went and did not return;
Then the tears in my eyes would burn:

But really what I'm trying to say is that
I love them both in every way.

*Tara Kay*

## HERBY THE HOOVER

The cupboard door stands open and I can see inside
My mummy's tall black cleaner, he goes in there to hide.

I must be very careful what I drop on the ground.
My mummy says he eats the dirt and things that lie around.

Mum says she likes her Herby - I can't think what she means.
I 'spose it's 'cause he helps her when she polishes and cleans.

I don't like Herby Hoover when he comes on the scene.
Though every time he visits the place is sparkling clean.

I sometimes have a headache when mummy plugs him in.
He sounds as if he's angry and kicks up such a din.

One day when I was playing I dropped my favourite sweet.
So Herby had it for his lunch from there beneath my feet.

I cover up my tiny ears 'cause there is so much noise.
I run into my bedroom and stay there with my toys.

Sometimes he's really greedy and gobbles up a book.
My mummy gets quite angry and gives him such a look!

Then when he's filled his tummy the door is opened wide,
Mum takes him to the garden and cleans out his inside.

I'm always pleased when mummy packs Herby safe away.
She stands him in the cupboard ready for another day . . .

*A Constable*

## MAN ALONE

Man is a special person,
One who stands alone.
His aura surrounds him.
The world has yet to know
Of his fearsome pride, and
Heart of gold.

He's a knight in shining armour
And, beneath it boyish sulks
He could fly to the Moon,
Or just drown in black despair.
Strong, dark and brooding,
For to catch a female eye.
But, is he the stronger sex?
I have to reason why.

*Mary E Wain*


## SAN JUAN

Sky as blue as sapphire
Water ripples and glistens in the sun
A boat passes slowly by
A fisherman searching for crabs
Boats in the harbour
The smell of fresh caught fish
We sit and watch life go by
Time to go and climb up to the mountains
As dusk is creeping in
We sit and watch the sun go down
Time to go another day has gone

*Janet Childs*

## LOVE LEAVING EARLY

The gaiety of balloons
in a darkened room
Give pleasure to the eye.
So what makes thoughts
turn to the end of life?
Memories of pleasure are few
as love turns to hate.
Cold outside -
Set within the room.
No hope to go forward
Promise of spring - forbidden
As snow swirls against
tight shut window.
A flutter of paper
in the empty passageway
Mocks the rattle of the door.
For the balloons have deflated
And so has life
With a gentle sigh
Why? Hangs in the air
As the petals of roses
from above softly cry.

*Sandra E Kirton*


## CHARNWOOD FOREST

The menhir still towers on a lonely hill
This ancient stone so tall and grey
There since time and the world began
Still pristine, as before dinosaur or man.

The rock that saw the village by the lake
From Lough to busy market town
It was covered in moss the day before
But, I scraped it clean that day.

I could see for miles; there were none insight
I carved her name in the stone,
It was evening and in a fading light
But, I worked on there alone.

From whence or where, I scarcely know,
How the tempest came or blew,
I've left the memory for all to see
On the menhir, that towers, on a lonely hill.

*Harry Glover*


## MY NUMBER ONE

There's lots of teddies everywhere,
Some have patches, some have no hair.
But one is missing, where has he gone
He's my favourite, my Number One.
Last time I looked he was there
Sitting in his favourite chair.
I've looked in the cupboard and under the bed
I wished he'd told me, I wished he'd said.
It's very lonely without him here
He's such a lovely little bear.
With a nice soft fur and cuddly too;
Oh! Number One I do miss you.
What shall I do at the end of the day
Why dear teddy did you go away?
What shall I do when I go to bed
And you're not on the pillow next to my head?
But listen! What's that, did I hear someone call?
Yes it's teddy he's not lost at all.
He's been helping mommy make the tea
Now we're together again, just him and me.

*Iris Taylor*

## LEFT ALL ALONE

Four walls, a window with just the light and the wind penetrating
through, a feeble old gentlemen sits in his chair, he now has nothing
to do

Yet 70 years on his heart keeps on beating, he keeps himself warm by
wrapping his legs in newspaper sheeting

He tries to move, he feels so stiff, arthritis couldn't afford to give this
gentleman a miss

He now carries a walking stick, which is welded to the palm of his
hand, which bears the inscription 'To be brave, is to stand'

As he tries to move, his legs take the pressure and his mind takes the
pain, he knows he must follow it though because if he didn't it would
perhaps be another hour or two

He finally stands, his back all crooked and bent, he struggles to the
window, but to him it's time well spent

He looks down the street and his eyes light up with joy, to see the
children playing which brings back memories back to when he was
just a boy

Then suddenly tears enter into his eyes, as the pain in his body came
as no surprise

He finally falls to the floor as his walking stick is released, never to be
grasped again, because now he is at peace

I write this poem in anger, yet with thought, let's look after the older
generation, the ones who now need our support.

*Christopher Newton*

## FOR I KNEW . . .

Love flared in my heart
As I heard her sing:
The melodious tilt of her throat
Took me on the wing
To paradise;
And only then did I really perceive
How lovely was her face:
A sort of shiver quivered my breast
Like the hot-aching embrace
Of virgin-pure ice;
For I knew, at once, that *our* paths
Never, never could meet:
She was some distant icon,
Whose voice, transporting me, fleet,
Must me for ever suffice . . .

*R John Austin*


## BLUEBELL CORNER

The bluebells are blooming in bluebell corner.
More blooms each day as the sun grows warmer
Its been the same for many a long year
But this year it's different with memories held dear.
Now re-vamped with pots, pebbles and stone
I stand in the garden all alone.
Should stand back with pride and say 'I did that.'
But 'neath the bluebells and earth
Lies my beautiful cat.
Japonica now shades him from the hot summer sun.
My beautiful 'Wills' - the quiet one.

*Christine Anne Storer*

## THE BRIDAL GOWN

You never saw my family
You didn't see me grow
You wasn't at my wedding with my groom in tow.
You never saw my children,
You missed the best part of my life.
You saw me only as a child, but never as a wife.
I needed your expert opinions
I wanted you to be there,
To give me strength, to show me how,
To be a wife with a contented air.
I'm pleased you didn't see my father.
He looked all defeated and down,
But I would have loved you, to see me
In my long white bridal gown.

*Gwendolyn Morris*


## A CORNER OF COUNTY WATERFORD

Leaving Dungarvan in the dark and rain,
With a feeling that I will be there again
To see once more the mountains and the River Colligan,
The memories of these things linger on and on.

To go again to Waterford beside the sparkling quay,
Then there's the great crystal chandelier - what a sight to see.
Into the town with its shopping and its life,
See it as the night comes down, all shining with lights.

Then there was lovely little Lismore with its quiet charm,
Its peace and happiness you feel in its heart.
The rows of little houses all decked around with flowers,
I wanted to take it all back home and relive those peaceful hours.

*M Budrey*

# IN MEMORY OF AN OAKHAM SCHOOLMASTER

Had he allowed his heart to speak whilst waiting for his evening meal
those many barren years ago, (and times he wished it had been so),
how different might his life have been.
But Public School had made him proud and forwardness was not
                                                        allowed.
He sat there almost stiff with fright, this strange emotion bottled tight,
that she sat next to him that night.
'Have you been teaching here for long,' she asked.
And he replied 'Too long. My twentieth anniversary
Has been and gone. Don't be like me.
Marry yourself a nice young man and start a family while you can,
or soon you'll too be in a rut and vegetate, without the guts to make
                                                        a change.'
She spoke again . . .
'Young men are shallow, weak and vain. To trust them, is to suffer
pain' she said. Then gently touched his hand, to try to make him
understand that though his hair was turning grey, his soul was youthful
as the day that he'd arrived with hopes held high, and cloudless as a
summer sky to her. For in his company, she felt a longed for harmony.
All this within his heart he heard, though she spoke not another word.
He knew what his reply should be, instead, he sat there silently.
His heart was racing nonetheless, but could not bring himself to press
her fingers, thus to let her know how much he wished it could be so.
She stood, and kissed him tenderly, then from his life walked sadly free.
This seed of joy was never sown. He died retired, remote, alone.
        Januarius

*Gerald Botteley*

## Unity - Home - School

I dreamt I stood in a studio
And watched the sculptors there.
The clay they used was a young child's mind
And they fashioned it with care.

One was a teacher; the tools he used
Were books and music and art;
One a parent with a guiding hand
And a gentle loving heart.

Day after day the teacher toiled
With a touch that was loving and sure,
While the parents laboured by his side
And polished and smoothed it o'er.

And when at last their work was done
They were proud of what they had wrought
For the things they had moulded into the child
Could neither be sold or bought.

And each agreed that he would have failed
If he had worked alone
For behind the parent stood the school
And behind the teacher the home.

*Robert Joseph Coburn*


## Advice

The setting, burnished copper sun
said languidly 'Life goes on.'
The cedar avenue reached the skies
and whispered 'There will be other eyes.'
In the grove the crickets chirped their call,
incessantly repeating 'Time heals all.'

*Rebecca de Warenne*

## THE PATH THROUGH THE FIELDS

For many years I've trod this path
Through fields where Farmer Long made hay
By hand, with scythe, and often talked
Of how life was in his young day.

Now he is gone and all has changed,
But still I tread the same straight track
I've walked along since I was young.
My memory often takes me back.

The fields have now become a marsh,
And willow trees have changed the scene.
Marsh marigolds and ladysmock
With ragged robin too are seen.

In spring the frogs invade the place,
Their constant croaking sound is heard.
But still the path remains the same,
Though all these changes have occurred.

In Roman times this track was here,
Part of a saltway so I'm told.
And traders walked along it then,
This path is, therefore, very old.

Thus past and present come together,
The path is like a memory lane.
Much time has passed since I first walked
Where I still hope to walk again.

*Kay Gilbert*

## MOBILE PHONE

Tring, tring,
Ring, ring - cling
To your mobile phone,
So never to be not at home;

Links across miles
With happy word smiles,
As new technology enables -
Far more immediacy than previous cables!

Always on call,
Without chance to stall,
An ever continuing present -
By not being physically present;

So's not to have to hesitate
To communicate -
Thus furthering the wow
Of the 'immediate now'!

Ever eyeing one person
While hearing another's version -
Ones immediate companion declined,
Due to having another in mind;

And what a strange notion
To realise the airwaves commotion,
Traversing all through and around,
Without slightest visible sound -
Whizzing about throughout the land,
Awaiting the slight of hand
That dials the number -
That disturbs your peaceful slumber . . .

Tring, tring, ring, ring!

*Paul Bartlett*

# NATURE

It's so uplifting when you see
a beautiful flower or a leafy tree,
or wend your way down a narrow lane
with banks of foxglove and fleabane.
There may be a cottage with roof of thatch,
that is so pretty it makes your breath catch,
or perhaps a robin singing sweetly there,
and the scent of roses wafting in the air.
All these things are there to see
and for everyone they are free.
We must be thankful for nature's best
and realise how much we're blest.

*Mary McPhee*

# MUSIC

Often it's a song
A snatch of music, loud.
Transports me back ten years
When I was younger and proud.
I smile without realising
Thoughts pop into my head.
All night partying, drinks,
No commitment - enough said.
My smile fades with the music
I look about me.
I'd escaped for three minutes
For a while my eyes didn't see.

*Jane Manning*

## No Choice

We had to go to war . . . we had no choice,
For the horrors that we saw quite choked our voice.
The slaughter of a race - day after day
Was more than we could face and words could not convey
The images of bloody deeds . . . the weeping women's cries
A desperate peoples' needs . . . we could not just stand by.
We had to join the fight against this heinous foe
And strive for what we know is right - or let it go . . .

> The right to raise our children, without fear
> To cherish all we have - which we hold dear.
> To feel the breeze and warmth of morning sun
> And not be looking down the muzzle of a gun.
> To smell the flowers and see the patchwork fields
> And not be used as pawns and *human shields!*
> To allow nature in her wisdom to decide
> Our length of years . . . not Genocide!

They do not deserve the bombing of their towns
The razing of their villages and burning of their homes.
The murder of their menfolk, the raping of their wives
The brutality and oppression that robs them of their lives.

We hear their silent pleading - a quiet, simple cry
'Please . . . someone help us . . . don't just stand by
And watch once more - a genocide.
What if it was your . . . ? You must decide.'

*Yes . . . we had to go to war*
*We had no choice!*

**Chris Cox**

# FAMILY

As I sit here and let my thoughts float
I realise what my own family means.
Family I guess means a whole lot to me
What can I say . . .
It's as simple as this
My mum whom I love and adore
Who has taught me that there is nothing wrong in wanting more
More from life, more from myself.
Everytime I reach out for her
I know she will always be there.
My dad whom I respect ever so much
has been a great role model to follow.
As wise as he is . . .
Has always told me to stand up for myself
Don't let anything get in the way
Do your best
and everything else will fall into its place.
How true their words have been.
Moving on I must not forget my siblings.
Quarrels, laughs, tears, joys, arguments, secrets, friendships
are just some of the things we have experienced together.
Together we have all learned, bonded and grown up stronger.
Many more good, bad, hard, enjoyable and testing times will
                                        come our way
We'll all pull through stronger, wiser and more appreciable I am sure.
My family is not perfect
but in my very own eyes they are nothing less.
It's hard to express my feelings.
What I have said so far is just the beginning.
My family as a whole is my friend
I do know they will have a special place in my heart always.

*Shazma Begum*

## FRIDAY NIGHT

Friday night at our house was a grand affair;
We pushed back the sofa and the armchair.
For I remember as a child, we had to make the space
to bring the big zinc bath inside, and put it in place.

The water was all bubbling on the kitchen range;
The children nowadays would think it very strange
to bath on the hearth by firelight.
To be the first in was usually a fight!

By the time the second child climbed in
the water felt quite cool to the skin.
Mum would bustle through with a new supply
saying 'Mind your legs or you'll get burnt and cry.'

When the last was out, and the bath moved away,
emptied and hung in the shed on a nail till next Friday.
We would all sit round the fire with cocoa in hand.
One happy family saying, 'Bath nights are grand!'

*Shirley Travis*


## TELEPATHY

Blow me a smoke-ring
        fill it with smiles
Continuous smoke-rings
        to cover the miles
Let your heart drift
With the love of
        our Lord
Carried in spirit to
        my tiny abode.

Wispy the wings of
            your Angel Divine
Bearing your message
            of beautiful rhymes
Sealing a friendship
With love oh so true
Continuous smoke-rings
I'll send back to you.

*Mary Skelton*


## NAN AND MR TIBBS

Nan sank down wearily on the bus seat
Thankful to take the weight off her feet.
Her shopping bags heavy, and she didn't feel strong
She will soon be home tho' - it will not take too long.

Nan thought of Mr Tibbs by the door keeping watch
Waiting to hear the key in the latch.
Mr Tibbs would come running, tail held high
She would stoop to stroke him, but the pain, oh my!

Boil the kettle, tea will soon be ready
Must be extra careful, as hands now unsteady.
The cat will understand tho' and make the most
Of warming his tum, whilst Nan makes some toast.

The fire will crackle and burn so bright
As they settle down for another night.
They have been together for a number of years
Have shared lots of fun, and shed a few tears.

When tea is done and they have eaten their fill
The cat still has in store, another thrill.
Mr Tibbs will wait until Nan pats her lap
Then joyfully jump on for another cat-nap.

*Marie Brown*

## A FAIRY STORY

Xmas is coming, money running out
'No fancy presents this year,' I shout.
Every year my intentions are good
I'll start buying early, I know I really should.
Nothing in the pantry, fridge is quite bare
as into the empty freezer I stare.
I don't wish for fortunes, furs or the like
just enough to buy Katie, Becky and Bill - a bike.
Maybe a jumper for Mark
one he would only dare to wear in the dark.
Susie and Deb a negligée I think
something in a nice shade of pink.
Nice warm long john's to keep Eddie warm
great to wear while out in a storm.
All of these things wouldn't cost the earth.
Who knows perhaps the good fairy
*will fill up my purse!*

*K Hines*


## ELECTRO-MOTIVE FORCE CONDUCTORS
## OR PYLONS OVER THE A1

Gigantic rigid monsters
heads erect, like arrogant slaves
striding the land,
rope-linked with high-voltage wires.

Majestic skeletal leviathans
incompatible with our countryside.
Metal pylons,
successful captive invaders
of green magnetic fields.

*Terri Annable*

## LIGHT A CANDLE

The flame flickers, the candle burns down,
The lights go out, all round the town.
There's someone watching and waiting to see,
If we'll remember him above - both you and me.

I mean our God, who's always forever about.
If we say a prayer, we can find him out.
Lots of people kneel and say just a few words.
A big thank you for this life and all the birds.

Some people are lucky, they haven't got a care
and couldn't be bothered if God is out there.
But many rely on him nearly all of the time
I think of him now while I'm writing this rhyme.

New candles are made to give off good light,
We can see when we're wrong and know when we're right.
Whatever our Creed, whoever we may be
If we believe in Jesus, we'll all be able to see.

So when you light a candle just say a little prayer
And he will guide you here, there and everywhere.
A candle of light, a flame of burning desire
Someone very lonely just sitting by the fire.

All those candles, some are coloured others are white,
Just remember Jesus and do everything that is right.
Tell him you love him and pray every now and then
You'll have a happier time, when you light a candle again.

*Will Of Endon*

## THE PLOVER'S TALE

Staring through the cloud's soft weave
I watched in pleasured awe
The lapwing soaring high above
The unforgiving shore
Searching out each hard won meal
Fighting hunger's battle
Casting shadows on the backs
Of sinewed, bone-thin cattle
Hasten on then kinder season
Bring sustenance from dearth
Realise her reason
For being on this earth
To generate her line again
Through every fledgling treasure
Provide us with a lasting train
Of such exquisite pleasure.

*Steph Needham*


## NEVER VOLUNTEER

Never volunteer,
I was informed,
Working the typewriter,
Would I, volunteer?
But, yes I did.

It was an experience,
I wanted to try,
Oh, how happy,
It had made me,
To know that someone,
Somewhere, will gain,
Some strength from,
The sense of charity.

When they know people,
Really care,
They have new life,
Everywhere, volunteer.

*B Brown*


## A BALL

I am a ball, a rubber ball,
I crawl and jump, I soar and fall,
and sometimes crash into a wall,
      which chance chose to erect.
I'm tossed about on life's playground;
when kicked - pit in, and then rebound;
roll on, lie still - till the next round,
      on terms I don't elect.

When struck - from my tormentor fly,
his schemes to foil, will to defy,
a goal to find in friendly sky,
      a vantage point to gain.
I won't waste time to settle old score.
Instead I'll open a new door
to seek out truth, and not ignore,
      its wisdom pure and plain.

Soon in my cosy paradise
I'll learn above base things to rise,
and cease to fear fate's tiresome dice
      of its capricious mood.
Then I alone will thus decide
whether to run, or swim, or glide,
to get good fortune on my side,
      no more to sigh and brood.

*George Hebda*

## THE TAMWORTH TWO

Two Tamworth ginger pigs went on the run,
They didn't think the abattoir would be much fun.
They escaped and ran like hell,
That's why I have this tale to tell.
The thought of bacon, belly pork and liver,
sent them racing for the river.
The River Avon could be deep and wide,
but Butch and Sundance reached the other side.
They led the folk a merry dance,
against gun and dart they stood no chance.
But there is a sequence to this story,
of Sundance and his mate.
For now they have been adopted,
and life for them is great.

*Tom Grocott*


## ENGLAND, ENGLAND

Attack, attack the Hun, my boys,
Legions heed the nation's cry,
Brothers, base men, mortals all,
Irreparable bodies lie,
On blood-sapped lea,
Non-coms left to die.

Advance, engage the foe,
Let no man hear your cry,
Brave hearts are needed now,
Is there a heaven in the sky,
Or is Earth a lasting Hell?
Now Lord, please reply!

*Alan Dawes*

# PRECIOUS

My life has been enriched by a visit from the USA.
My vocabulary certainly widened, it extended day by day.
I already knew the usual ones like instead of 'zed' they say 'zee.'
But when they didn't know what a fortnight was it really tickled me.
I didn't know I used a faucet. It took a while to switch on.
And instead of saying 'cheerio' I remembered to say 'so long.'
I drew the drapes each evening so the sidewalk couldn't be seen,
And we learnt all about their president and they about our queen.
They looked a little oddly when I said I was dying for a fag,
I offered them around though, then popped them in my bag,
Of course, it was a purse to them, I forgot to mention that.
And when we filled with petrol, they asked the man for gas.
They took the spare out of the trunk to check that it was fine
Then after choosing candy, stood patiently in line.
They kept on wanting the bathroom, cleaner people I'd never met,
But when I went to change the towels, none of them were wet!
A word that was their favourite, always said in that American way
Was that under used word, precious, and we heard it every day.
The world it was so precious, gifts, places, bottles of Chardonnay
And after a few glasses of the stuff, it was the only world they
                                                    could say.
They used it with such drama, we could tell it was sincere.
They said it so loud and forceful, everyone could hear.
Precious days passed here in England, then they returned to the USA,
So until our next vacation, be sure to have a nice day!

*Josephine Burnett*

# FATE

He bows his head against the rain with his coat pulled tight
in his heart he knows, it will be a long, wet night.

He's been walking all day around the streets of the town,
looking for something to eat, but no one helps you when
you're down.

The shoes on his feet are sodden and worn,
his coat is too big, it's dirty and torn.

The trousers he found, tied round his waist with a rope,
when you look into his eyes you can see there's no hope.

He searches the doorways for somewhere to rest,
somewhere dry perhaps, or out of the wind at best.

It's a pitiful sight to see him slumped on the floor,
a bundle of dirty wet rags, a proud man no more.

It shouldn't be so in a world full of wealth,
We should all have food, clothes and our health.

But alas, that's not so, those with wealth won't always share,
they look after themselves, for the rest they don't care.

The results you can see in any town you choose,
it's full of desperate people slumped in doorways
with holes in their shoes.

But what's the point of grabbing all you can,
leaving the rest to struggle by,
not sharing, not helping,
you can't take it with you when you die.

So as you go through life try and help your fellow man,
don't be one of those who turn their backs, give a little if you can.

Remember, you never know what fate has in store,
it could be you one day, slumped on a cold, wet floor.

*J Addis*

## THOUGHTS OF HOME

My thoughts go drifting back to as a child of two or three
I must have been around that age, as by my father's knee
I stood quite close to him, and he with his strong arm held me.
Close by, my elder brother sat. I can see him still, but as I muse
I wonder was it Jack or was it Bill?

Home then for us meant happy days, I visualise it all
The wireless on the table, the pictures on the wall.
The poker on the fireplace, the mantelpiece so tall.
My dad, he told us stories, and usually of some ghost
And then we laughed with him and wondered who was
frightened most.

This was my home, and love was there, we took it in our stride
I can't explain it really, but I felt the love inside.
Home then to us was aye sae dear, there was no sad times -
All was cheer.

These thoughts of past days, thoughts of home
Are thoughts of love intense.
I know now that they're both entwined
Somehow it all makes sense.
Yes! Home is where the heart is.
The theme that's set by you.
Over sentimental?
But believe me - it is true.

**S Izzard**

## NO-MAN'S-LAND

So much pain, grief and sorrow,
The violence is never ending,
A tyrannical man, with a backing
Of force and prejudices.
People rise up and fight back,
Does anyone have a care
For all those in the middle
A spacious field . . . 'No Man's Land',
Full of helpless men, women and children.
With war there are no winners,
Only destroyers, hell-bent on
Coming up trumps over others.
What makes someone tick so?
No one really knows.
Heroes, there are all types.
Fighters on the side of good.
The families who forsake all,
Just to escape with their loved ones.
Children, so resilient despite their
Innocence being shattered so cruelly.
I long for an ideal, for fight to cease,
For people to try and all coexist.
I pray for peace and harmony
So fighters are able to go back to families,
The refugees to go home, live in safety,
For the children to laugh once again.

*Nasima Ali*

## FIELDBANK FARM

The fields have gone now, and the harvest mouse
that used to scamper up the golden corn,
and in their place, a new 'Mock Tudor' house
with timbers aged to make them seem time-worn.

Beside it stands another just the same
and on and on in serried rows they stand.
Where once red poppies set the land aflame
red bricks are planted by some builder's hand.

With names like 'Badger Walk' and 'Roedeer Drive'
tarmac chokes the fertile soil beneath.
The lark has lost the battle to survive,
its nest devoured by JCB's sharp teeth.

The farmhouse too has long since been destroyed
along with outhouse, barn and milking parlour.
Now the supermarket fills the void
with Spanish plums, mangetout from Guatemala.

School-running mums in shiny four-wheel drives
pull into neatly white-lined parking spaces.
Designer clad, the new young country wives
with lipstick smiles and salon sunbed faces.

They boast of their new houses with such pride
'Four beds, two baths and burglar alarm'.
To build dream homes they kill the countryside
so they can claim to live at Fieldbank Farm.

*Glen Dann-Gibbons*

## A WALK IN THE WOODS

I walked alone in the woods today
'Neath a canopy of leaves
that shaded me from the sun's bright rays,
But dappled golden patterns on my way.
I heard the chattering of the birds,
And breathed the scent of flowers.
The rustle of furry creatures hiding away
To come out again at the close of day.
I heard the chuckle of the tiny stream
As it rippled down by the meadow
And frogs creaked their mating theme
from out of the muddy hollows.
Startled squirrels leapt from tree to tree,
Their tails like banners flying free.
Shy little violets and primroses sweet
And a carpet of bluebells at my feet.
How I loved my walk 'neath the trees,
For the peace and tranquillity it gave to me.

*Emma Hunt*


## VISIONS IN CLOUDS

High above, white steeds of the skies
Stables unknown far beyond abides
Riderless rein, the hidden hand
Eager to race o'er distant land.

Wind in pursuit, unwilling relent
Onward ever onward, till passion spent
Iconic portraits appear in view
Castles, angels, yet visions anew.

Dale, meadow, steeple and stream
Images above these, their mists seen
Journeys endless till their demise
Lost forever white steeds of the skies.

*H Taylor*


## LULLABY

Sing lula, sing lula,
Sing a song and rest your precious head,
Sing lula, sing lula,
Sing a note and slip into your bed.
Sing darkness, sing nightfall
I will be your shining star.
Just close your eyes, and wish a wish,
We'll journey home so far.

Sing lula, sing lula,
My voice will carry off your fear.
Sing lula, sing lula,
My melody will bring you near.
Sing angel, sing slumber,
The harmony, mother's kiss.
A cherub song, a cupid trill,
The night time hymn we'll miss.

Sing lula, sing lula,
As night time comes to end.
Sing lula, sing lula,
The morning sun it sends.
Sing stardust, sing moon beam,
Now let my babe's wish fly,
And I will wait another hour
To sing my lullaby.

*H Beddoes*

## REMINISCENCE

The millennium day will soon arrive,
January first, 1906 was my birthday,
So I am lucky to be alive,
To enjoy celebrations in a special way.
I have lived sixty-four years in my present abode,
Neighbours coming and going, bringing up their young,
The children allowed to play in the road.
Well brought up, knowing right from wrong,
Thinking of the horrors of the first world war,
Living alone, tending my home and son.
Domestic life with husband and child
Was all I waited for.
Now at last this time had come, I could not ask for more.
Hectic modern life with no time to spare,
For working wives to organise needs much thought and care,
Husbands who offer to assist with chores are really very wise,
Togetherness brings happiness on which most families thrive.

*E Ballard*


## PASTURES NEW

We both finished work at sixty,
they have put us both out to graze.
She has finished emptying bedpans
and I've finished those track working
days.

Family and friends, sympathetic, and
'How will you cope?' they all sigh.
But she has her own work's pension
and I've got a little put by.

We were both up early this morning,
as my old mates walked to work
in the rain.
I'm looking up the road
for a taxi . . .
'Cause we're booked on the
eight-thirty plane!

*Jeff Edwards*


## INVITATION TO A WALK

Dally a while,
With your smile,
And tell me you would like to go
To the woods where the bluebells grow.

I will take you by the hand
To the magical land
And we can stroll by the stream
And wonder at this springtime dream.
See the lovely blossom bloom
Like confetti suspended in the womb
Of this tender season of spring:
This annual miracle to which we sing
Praise upon praise in grateful love
Of such wonderful gifts from above.

And at the setting of the sun,
When our time will have run,
We can look back and say
Wasn't that a beautiful day.

*J T Purdom*

# FORGET ME NOT

If you ever go to Flanders,
Where fields of poppies grow,
And gaze upon the headstones,
Aligned up in a row.

Remember there's a soldier,
In every little plot,
They lie there for a reason,
They gave us all they'd got.

They were fighting for our freedom,
That we might live in peace,
They were fighting for our freedom,
In hope that wars might cease.

For when you see those poppies,
They'll make you very sad,
Each represents a soldier,
Who gave up all he had.

Now he can't walk in England,
Down any country lane,
Or smell the fields and hedgerows,
Washed clean by summer rain.

Nor see the flowers in springtime,
When gardens they all fill,
Or taste the fruits of autumn,
Or feel the winter's chill.

He hopes you will remember,
He paid the total price,
That we might live and prosper,
Don't waste his sacrifice.

All he asks come each November,
It doesn't cost a lot,
To wear with pride your poppy,
And please forget-me-not.

*D Wheatley*

## A QUICK CHANGE OF LIFE

Out on the driveway, duster in hand,
Adrenaline pumping, feeling just grand.
Your bike it was gleaming, leathers fit snug,
Speed-hungry hubby, with a big, bad, bike, bug.
Away for the weekend, with the motorbike crew,
Racing and chasing, overtaking a few.
Bye then my darling, a kiss with a frown,
You say you'll be careful, but you'll get your knee down.
Well, you certainly did it, your slider was marked,
But another kind of journey have you now embarked.
How could you have known that fateful April day,
That three months later in a bed you would lay.
Multiple injuries, the doctor had said,
Back is broken, lucky he's not dead.
The pain and the sorrow, how long will it last,
How could it be worthy of a 100 mph blast.

*Sue Knight*

# HOBBIES

Why not try a hobby like crocheting or knitting,
Better to occupy yourself, than to be bored just sitting.
Try painting or give thought to reading,
What you will achieve you hardly will be believing.

To pacify my friends I bought a knitting pattern,
Maybe, with progress, my hobby it could earn
Enough to pay for other things, soon I'd be adept
At making my winter clothes, so my mind was set.

With pattern on the table, needles in my hand,
I followed the instructions to knit a woollen band.
I knitted one, purled one, right to the very end,
Needles were awkward, they would not bend.

Determinedly I knitted on, my garment growing large,
Dropping stitches, picking up, my task was very hard.
The wool became tangled, the cat joined in the fun,
I thought, if this is knitting, shall be glad when I've done.

What I did not understand when I cast off at last,
Pulled the jersey over my head, all my hopes were dashed.
That carefully knitted sweater, fitted like a sack
Down to my knees in front, halfway up my back.

To console my disappointment and to prove I could,
Tried my hand at carving little pieces of wood.
It looked easy in the book, showing diagrams and plans,
Telling about trees in far-off foreign lands.

I set out my tools on the table there,
They looked so lethal, really made me stare,
Decided to make an elephant to please the child next door,
All I did was cut my thumb, it was so very sore.

I chipped away, my efforts were very poor,
The only things that grew were the shavings on the floor.
My fingers cut and bleeding with bandages galore,
I resembled a casualty returning from a war.

Then I joined an artist's class to paint a picture fine,
On a river's bank we sat in a long, straight line.
With easel in front of me, palette board at hand,
I gazed on the outlook, on the green and pleasant land.

I tried to concentrate on the river's silver sheen,
On the dancing shadows cast by the sunlight's gleam,
But I was attacked by marauding mosquitoes,
Frogs sitting on my brushes and clothes.

My finished creation was a riot of colour,
Picasso had nothing on me, but my tutor
Gazed in horror, murmured unspeakable things
About my tree trunks and my swan's wings.

From time to time my interest I have turned
To making lampshades and sewing, but I have learned
My talents are not creative, no matter how I try,
In future, I shall watch television and let the world go by.

*Lois Burton*

## THE POWER OF THE MIND

Thought that transcends reaches now perceived
Passing above the barriers of time
An insight propelled into realms now eclipsed
With an invisible link that unites the past,
                the present and the future.

The power of imagination, foresight and inner awareness
From a soul restless in its entirety, searching for
                the truth
Or inner calm that floats above, and beyond,
        but always out of reach, defying capture
Until the power of the mind is stilled.

But then we have no man at all - just an empty shell
                and forgotten dreams
The flame extinguished and only ash.

*Doris Hoole*


## AUTUMN

Autumn is coming; the leaves start to fall,
Down come the branches, blossom and all,
The stars are just fading, way up in the air,
But still their sheer beauty glows everywhere!
I look at the 'curtains' which dance in the sky,
And wonder why heaven seems always too high -
For mortals like me to arise to its height,
But one day I'll see it and ascend in the night!
When wintertime comes and summer is o'er,
The autumn will vanish for one year more.
So I'll live till the sunshine comes back once again,
And try to put up with all of the rain.

*Sharon Howells*

## MY ROVING MIND

Alone in my room, my mind is free
To travel the world, or in harness be.
It can think of the pain and suffering around
Or can delve into joys so often to be found.
It can muddle thoughts up like a jigsaw of wood
Or can clarify statements, just as it should.
It can plan for the future or remember the past
Or just to this moment hold doggedly fast.
It's free to criticise people, or 'join' them in joy
Though far better the latter - it doesn't want to annoy.
Thoughts can lead to words, so more useful to think
Of only the best, and from unkind thoughts shrink.
If it thinks of its loved ones now departed this earth
My mind could feel sad - but there were times of mirth
With so much enjoyment and love to remember
My mind should be happy from New Year to December.
But my mind can be serious, and that's only right
For life for all people can be quite a fight
Perhaps I'll think of something to help someone along
My tiny thoughts into action may make them more strong.
Only God really knows what my mind should be doing
Today, as I sit here, am I His thoughts construing
For that is the way to use my free thought
To the betterment of all - then thoughts won't come to nought
Alone - what a privilege - my thoughts put into prayer
It's good to use quiet times for clearing the air
Of all that is wrong at this time in my mind
There is so much that is good to think of I find.

*Muriel I Tate*

## AZURE FLIGHT

Black wings, cream body, crimson head,
Curving in joyful flight;
Half circles, quadrants,
With no cry.
Soundless joy in the summer air
Reaches me standing there
On hard brown clay.

Harsh line of plane streaks above,
Silver wings gleaming.
Reflecting,
Heat, sun, majesty.
Engines beat with power.
They lack the ease shown
By a bird.

*J England*